Vade Mecum

(n.) a needed thing carried around everywhere; a useful handbook or guidebook always kept on one's person; lit. "go with me"

C. JoyBell C.

The Three Flights emblem seen in various places within the pages of this book was materialized for the person of the author and it's worldwide copyright remains solely with her. Emblem the creation of R. DC. G.

All books by C. JoyBell C. are printed in the U.S.A., Great Britain and Continental Europe.

ISBN: **1492827010**
ISBN- **978-1492827016**

www.cjoybellc.com
authorcjoybellc@gmail.com

This book is dedicated to everyone who has fallen down, scraped his or her knee, laughed at a stupid thing and found joy in the magic of the ordinary. Also to those who reach for answers and revelations— may you find them all here!

To my son... you know you are tattooed onto my heart (which is good because I know you wouldn't want me to have a tattoo of your face on my arm...)

Contents

Foreword

October 3, 2013
San Antonio, Texas

Some places in this world make you feel wise. Locations of natural beauty, where you feel connected to the effortless immensity of the land or the sea. Sites of human artistry or achievement, where some imagined potential has been made into reality.

There is a picture that many would assume is a picture of C. JoyBell C., which would become my very first encounter with her. In the photograph, a beautiful woman sits looking out across the Mediterranean, her long white dress liquid in the wind, a stretch of the Italian coastline to her left, cut-stone archways rising above her. Almost everything about the photograph draws the eye toward this woman, from the composition of the image, to the contrast of that dress against the stony shadows around it, from the flawless curve of her cheek to her raven-dark hair to the line of the horizon cleaving the world in half at the far edge of sight.

But while she is in the picture, it is not a picture *of* her. Looking at this photograph, knowing that she saw what I saw, I also knew that she saw more. Her view had no obstructions — no columns, no walkway, no curved arches of cut stone. And no graceful, poised woman, either. The movement of her dress in the wind must surely have made her aware of her own physicality, but her form did not constrain her view as it did mine. What did that wider perspective show to her that lay beyond my narrower one? Without seeking out that precise spot, traveling across the world to reach it, and duplicating her position, I could not know. Yet even then, I *would* not know. Because everything about her pose and bearing said, "I am looking … not to search, but to see. Not to find but to know."

It is the picture of a moment. And my understanding of that hit me at a glance, in an instant— far less time than it's taken me to write these words or you to read them. Who could resist such a clarion call to understanding? When we look at it we are taken to that place, that time. We smell the sea air. We glory in the blue sky above and around us. We become that archetypally perfect woman, so that even if we have never worn a dress in our lives, never set a foot in Europe, we now know how the soft caress of fabric would grace our skin at the command of an Italian breeze. And while we cannot tell exactly what the person in this image is thinking or feeling, we think and feel with her. She stands in for us at an instant of beauty and welcomes us into her experience.

In very short order after stumbling across this picture, I found and read one of her first books, wrote a somewhat frenetic review of it, exchanged a few blog comments with her … and then watched with a very gratified spirit as her Facebook following and list of publications grew and grew. Eventually the day came when one of her quotes popped up in my newsfeed — not because I was following her page, but because one of my friends had shared it, completely independent of my connection to its author!

Why have all the observations and allusions and expressions in this book found their way around the globe? For the same reason that that picture had such an impact on me: wisdom is different from thought or insight. We all have our insights. We all put together original thoughts, at least from time to time. But wisdom isn't created; it is recognized. We find it in places and people and words. And once recognized, it can be shared.

Which I think is what makes this book special. It consists of understandings that have now been thrice shared. First when the author sent them out into the world, then when others recognized their truth, and now, all brought together as a result of their reflection back to their author and her desire to continue sharing what others have recognized as worthy.

There are places in this world that connect you to the ages, places where existence speaks to you, where you understand that wisdom is not created; only brought forward into recognition. C. JoyBell C. has a talent for finding those places — not just in far-flung or exotic locations, but everywhere! And she has a gift for recognizing wisdom, and for expressing it in ways that help others recognize it as well.

So that picture is not a picture of C. JoyBell C., just as this book is not a collection of her thoughts. Rather, they are both the means by which she shares the greater world with us and reminds us how to look and see it.

Mirrors and windows and photographs are not, in the end, all that different. Let's look and see what we can see.

Herb Mallette

Author Herb Mallette works as editor for an educational publishing company. He lives with his wife, four children, a beagle, basset hound and a cat. Once upon a time, he was a political news junkie until he swore off the whole occupation due to modern American politics being, according to him, "so disastrously depressing."

Introduction

Being quoted the world over and translated into languages such as French, Catalan, Russian, Spanish, Afrikaans, Portuguese, Slavic, Romanian, Chinese, Czech and Indonesian, while appearing in theses at Universities; in medical books authored by doctors like Dr. Randie Gottlieb, Multicultural Ed. Specialist and Dr. Kevin Lau, Chiropractor and Master of Holistic Nutrition (to name just a few); on twitter accounts of celebrities such as Donna Karan, Paris Hilton and Ashley Greene; on clothing brands in countries like Pakistan and Nepal; on television by such well-known personalities like Alan Colmes, American radio and television host, liberal political commentator for the Fox News Channel, host of TV show "Hannity & Colmes"; on beauty and perfume official websites such as the International Perfume Foundation;

to being quoted by beauty contestants during beauty pageants and women's rights activists at international conventions; humanitarian and child advocates; those working with the United Nations like Rev. Dr. Cindi Love, the Executive Director of Soulforce, who serves on the Faith and Religion Council for the Human Rights Campaign in Washington, D.C. and the Compass to Compassion global coalition— I have since come to the decision of compiling all of my words scattered across the globe and offering them up in a single, compact book!

I receive hundreds of emails from people all over the world— from Kathmandu to Bucharest to Brussels to New York City— I have received messages from the most obscure places on the planet, to the most iconic ones. All of these people write to me for the same reason: to express their gratitude for having come across my words quoted in various places and having experienced a changed life as a result. Changed from the inside out.

I have received long letters from people who discovered themselves healed and recovered from substance abuse addictions and failing marriages, thanks to my words transforming their lives and inspiring them. I've heard from young girls on every continent on earth, about how my writings have given them inner strength, the willpower to believe in themselves, the desire to change and grow for the better.

Who are my readers? My readers are teenagers in high school struggling to be better people despite any experiences they've had in life and where they come from; my readers are professionals in medical fields and astroengineers working for NASA. My readers are housewives who have a desire to raise the best kids they possibly can and soldiers who want to protect their countries to the best of their abilities! Artists, mystics and witches. Pastors, nuns and missionaries. Gay, bisexual, straight. My readers are your friends, your aunts and uncles, your mom, dad, your kids and you.

I had been thoroughly contemplating the idea of collecting my tidbit writings after coming across many books on Amazon wherein I am quoted by other authors— when I finally made the decision to create the book already, thanks to a very sincere message left on my Facebook Page timeline by a very dear fan and reader of my words, who said: "You're truly a great woman and I hope you continue to make such amazing quotes, because I feel that's what I admire about you the most— is the words you put— that explains so much about everyday life and sometimes they explain allot about how people in real life are. And it's all true." This particular fan, Preston, happens to be in high school and says that after his mother, I am his true inspiration. Having younger followers means so much to me and I have to admit that I value the younger generation with a much softer side of my heart, which is really what convinced me to gather my words and make this book, right away!

Vade Mecum is a Latin term which literally means "go with me" and was first used in 1629 to describe a handbook most needful— needful and useful enough to be attached to one's person at all times! Obviously, as the title indicates, I want this book to be a vade mecum for you, the reader. A vade mecum acting as a master key to unlock all doors, a torch to illuminate your nights and a healing balm to be applied and absorbed into your skin.

Always take me with you.

Livsnjutare

(n.) One who loves life deeply and lives it to the extreme.

I have come to accept the feeling of not knowing where I am going. And I have trained myself to love it. Alas, it is only when we are suspended in mid-air with no landing in sight, that we force our wings to unravel and begin our flight. And as we fly, we still may not know where we are going. But the miracle is in the unfolding of the wings. You may not know where you're going; but you know that so long as you spread your wings, the winds will carry you.

The only way that we can live is if we grow. The only way that we can grow is if we change. The only way that we can change is if we learn. The only way we can learn is if we are exposed. And the only way that we can become exposed is if we throw ourselves out into the open. Do it. Throw yourself.

You've got this life and while you've got it, you'd better kiss like you only have one moment, try to hold someone's hand like you will never get another chance to, look into people's eyes like they're the last you'll ever see, watch someone sleeping like there's no time left, jump if you feel like jumping, run if you feel like running, play music in your head when there is none and eat cake like it's the only one left in the world!

I'm unpredictable, I never know where I'm going until I get there, I'm so random, I'm always growing, learning, changing, I'm never the same person twice. But one thing you can be sure of about me: is I will always do exactly what I want to do.

I'm not in search of sanctity, sacredness, purity; these things are found after this life, not in this life; but in this life I search to be completely human: to feel, to give, to take, to laugh, to get lost, to be found, to dance, to love and to lust, to be so human.

I don't fit into any stereotypes. And I like myself that way.

Faith, love, trust and passion... these are things that seem to frighten people... yet these are the things that fuel my soul.

And I told him, I said: "One day you're going to miss the subway because it's not going to come. One of these days, it's going to break down and it's not going to come around and everyone else will just wait for the next one or will take the bus, or walk, or run to the next station: they will go on with their lives. And you're not going to be able to go on with your life! You'll be standing there, in the subway station, staring at the tube. Why? Because you think that everything has to happen perfectly and on time and when you think it's going to happen! Well guess what! That's not how things happen! And you'll be the only one who's not going to be able to go on with life, just because your subway broke down. So you know what, you've got to let go, you've got to know that things don't happen the way you think they're going to happen, but that's okay because there's always the bus, there's always the next station... you can always take a cab."

No, this is not the beginning of a new chapter in my life; this is the beginning of a new book! That first book is already closed, ended and tossed into the seas; this new book is newly opened, has just begun! Look, it is the first page! And it is a beautiful one!

Growing up means learning what life is. When you're little, you have a set of ideals, standards, criteria, plans, outlooks, and you think that you have to sit around and wait for them to happen to you and then life will work. But life isn't like that, for anybody; you can't fall in love with a standard, you have to fall in love with a person. You can't live in a criterion; you have to live your life. You can't wait for your plans to materialize, because they may never materialize the way you think they will. You can't wait to watch your ideals and standards walk up to you, because you cannot know what's yours until you have it. I always say: always take the first chance in case you never get a second one, but growing up takes that even one step further, growing up means that you have to hold on to what you have, when you have it, because what you have— that's yours and all the ideals and criteria you have set in your head— those aren't yours, because those haven't happened to you.

This is the key to life: To expect everything to be given to you from above, yet to be genuinely surprised and forever grateful, when they are. Expecting all good things to be yours, while not knowing how to take anything for granted. If there may be a key in life: this is the key.

What if you could pick one day of your life and everything would stop changing, every day would be similar and comparable to that one day, you'd always have the same people with you? If you could do that, would you do it? Would you pick that day and make that choice? We crave for things to stop changing; we wish that things would never change. But if we got what we wanted, there are so many things that are better, that we would never, ever know about. Sure, things would stay the same as that one wonderful day but then there would be nothing else out there, ever. So can you remember the very first day when everything really did begin to change? Is there a thing that can remind you? Mine is a blue rose, and that's when everything began to change because that's the day I began to believe in things I never believed in before; the day I found three blue roses. Think about your first day of change, can you remember all the new heights you've soared since that day? All the new people? All the better things and times? Would you throw all of that time away? I wouldn't. Instead, I want to finally accept all the things that I couldn't change, which led to me being right here, right now. Maybe we all carry around inside us one day we wish we could keep forever, something we wished never did change. It's time to let go of that day, and soar.

Destiny is real. And she's not mild-mannered. She will come around and hit you in the face and knock you over and before you know what hit you— you're naked— stripped of everything you thought you knew and everything you thought you didn't know and there you are! A bloody nose, bruises all over you and naked. And it's the most beautiful thing.

~ *The Conversation of Merachefet: A Book of Secrets*

I don't know why people are afraid of lust. Then I can imagine that they are very afraid of me, for I have a great lust for everything. A lust for life, a lust for how the summer-heated street feels beneath my feet, a lust for the touch of another's skin on my skin... a lust for everything. I even lust after cake. Yes, I am very lusty and very scary.

Life is a bowl of cherries. Some cherries are rotten while others are good; it's your job to throw out the rotten ones and forget about them while you enjoy eating the ones that are good! There are two kinds of people: those who choose to throw out the good cherries and wallow in all the rotten ones, and those who choose to throw out all the rotten ones and savor all the good ones.

I have realized that it is during the times I am far outside my element when I experience myself the most, that I see and feel who I really am, the most! I think that's what a comet is like, you see, a comet is born in the outer realms of the universe! But it's only when it ventures too close to our sun or to other stars that it releases the blazing "tail" behind it and shoots brazen through the heavens! And meteors become sucked into our atmosphere before they burst like firecrackers and realize that they're shooting stars! That's why I enjoy taking myself out of my own element, my own comfort zone and hurling myself out into the unknown. Because it's during those scary moments, those unsure steps taken, that I am able to see that I'm like a comet hitting a new atmosphere: suddenly I illuminate magnificently and fire dusts begin to fall off of me! I discover a smile I didn't know I had, I uncover a feeling that I didn't know existed in me... I see myself. I'm a shooting star. A meteor shower. But I'm not going to die out. I guess I'm more like a comet then. I am just going to keep on coming back.

I believe in going with the flow. I don't believe in fighting against the flow. You ride on your river and you go with the tides and the flow. But it has to be your river; not someone else's. Everyone has their own river and you don't need to swim, float, sail on theirs, but you need to be in your own river and you need to go with it. And I don't believe in fighting the wind. You go and you fly with your wind. Let everyone else catch their own gusts of wind and let them fly with their own gusts of wind, and you go and you fly with yours.

There are two things we should always be: 1. Raw, and 2. Ready. When you are raw, you are always ready and when you are ready you usually realize that you are raw. Waiting for perfection is not an answer, one cannot say "I will be ready when I am perfect" because then you will never be ready; rather, one must say "I am raw and I am ready just like this right now, how and who I am."

Politeness is okay but it gets old and boring. You want to attack life with a passion; not a politeness, you want people to think about you and remember you and say, "She is so passionate" you don't desire for people to think about you and remember you and say, "she is so polite," because, who cares about polite?

There are powers far beyond us, plans far beyond what we could have ever thought of, visions far more vast than what we can ever see on our own with our own eyes, there are horizons long gone beyond our own horizons. This is courage: to throw away what is our own that is limited and to thrust ourselves into the hands of these higher powers—God and Destiny. To do this is to abide in the realm of the eternal, to walk in the path of the everlasting, to follow in the footprints of God and demi-gods. The hardest part for man is the letting go. For some reason, he thinks himself big enough to know and to see what's good for him. But in the letting go... is found freedom. In the letting go... is found the flight!

A lifetime isn't forever, so take the first chance, don't wait for the second one! Because sometimes there aren't second chances! And if it turns out to be a mistake? So what! This is life! A whole bunch of mistakes! But if you never get a second chance at something you didn't take a first chance at? That's true failure.

There is a relationship between the eye contacts we make and the perceptions that we create in our heads, a relationship between the sound of another's voice and the emotions that we feel in our hearts, a relationship between our movements in space all around us and the magnetic pulls we can create between others and ourselves. All of these things (and more) make up the magic of every ordinary day and if we are able to live in this magic, to feel and to dwell in it— we will find ourselves living with magic every day. These are the white spaces in life, the spaces in between the written lines, the cracks in which the sunlight filters into. Some of us swim in the overflowing of the wine glass of life, we stand and blink our eyes in the sunlight reaching unseen places, we know where to find the white spaces, we live in magic.

I feel that we are often taken out of our comfort zones, pushed and shoved out of our nests, because if not; we would never know what we could do with our wings, we would never see the horizon and the sun setting on it, we would never know that there's something far better beyond where we are at the moment. It can hurt, but then later you say "thank you." I have been pushed and shoved and have fallen out and away so very, very, many, many times!

And others around me have not! But then, those others haven't seen what I have seen or felt what I have felt or been who I have been; they can't become what I have become. I am me.

Anything that you learn becomes your wealth, a wealth that cannot be taken away from you; whether you learn it in a building called school or in the school of life. To learn something new is a timeless pleasure and a valuable treasure. And not all things that you learn are taught to you, but many things that you learn you realize you have taught yourself.

It is beautiful to discover our wings and learn how to fly, flight is a beautiful process. But then to rest on the wings of God as He flies: this is divine.

Cake is happiness! If you know the way of the cake, you know the way of happiness! If you have a cake in front of you, you should not look any further for joy!

Never waste any amount of time doing anything important when there is a sunset outside that you should be sitting under!

It is when you lose sight of yourself, that you lose your way. To keep your truth in sight you must keep yourself in sight and the world to you should be a mirror to reflect to you your image. The world should be a mirror that you reflect upon.

"I have a dream."

"Is your dream very big?"

"No."

"Well is it very grand?"

"Not either."

"Neither?"

"Neither."

"What is it then?"

"It is very shiny."

It's like I get into a roller coaster and sit there while it goes up and down and upside down and sometimes I get thrown out and I hit my head, but I crawl back in again and the moment I'm back in, it just keeps on going and going again... all of this so I can find things out and then I write about the things I find out so you can find them out from me. All the bruises, all the wounds, all the bumps on the head, all the scars, just so I can take that and I can write all these things, and sometimes I say, "God, I don't want to be in this roller coaster anymore." But when I think about it; if I'm not right here, then where the hell would I be? On the sidewalk? I wasn't born to stand on the sidewalk; I was born to fly around crazy in the sky!

Why do we always begin to think about people when they die? I think we should think about people while they are still alive! That way, they can know that we're thinking about them! I always tell people when I'm thinking about them or that I thought about them or that I have been thinking about them, and it almost always scares them away, but so what, I am practicing the art of life and if that is frightening to them, then maybe they need to start living while they're still alive!

You get that one chance and damn it, you've got to take it! If there's one lesson I know I will take with me for eternity, its that there are those things that might happen only once, those chances that come walking down the street, strolling out of a café; if you don't let go and take them, they really could get away! We can get so washed out with a mindset of entitlement— the universe will do everything for us to ensure our happiness— that we forget why we came here! We came here to grab, to take, to give, to have! Not to wait! Nobody came here to wait! So, what makes anyone think that Destiny will keep on knocking on their door over and over again? It could, but what if it doesn't? You go and you take the chance that you get even if it makes you look stupid, insane, or whorish! Because it just might not come back again. You could wait a lifetime to see if it will... but I don't think you should.

"Do you really believe in destiny?"

"How can I not believe in Destiny, when there is no difference between my memories and my dreams at night? There's no difference between their reality. And if I dream something first, I remember it later when I am actually walking in the place or looking at the person I first dreamed of. Days later. Or years later. Destiny— she walks with me."

~ *The Conversation of Merachefet: A Book of Secrets*

"What does it mean if you tried to get somewhere but you didn't?"

"Like what?"

"Like if you were trying to get somewhere, but you couldn't find it? Does that mean something bad?"

"No. It doesn't mean something bad. It just means you have a second chance to do it. And two chances is always better than just one."

It is not needful for our dreams to be very grand nor very big. It is only needful for our dreams to be very shiny.

When I was in *Piazza di Spagna* in Rome, I watched (along with others) how many locals came to drink water from the fountain there. The people beside me said to each other "Oh my goodness, how disgusting, people just drink water from anywhere," while the whole time, I was thinking "Oh my goodness, how wonderful, people can just drink water from anywhere." We can be in the exact same place, looking at the exact same thing; but see that thing in a completely different way. You can go around the world and go to all the beautiful places; but never be happy, because happiness is something that you bring inside of you, it is not where you are or what you are looking at, but it is how you are and how you look at.

God and Destiny are not against us, rather, they are for us and they are the Ones who never forget the things we have long forgotten, the Ones who hear the desires of our heart that our own heads can't hear, and they are the Ones who never forget who we really are, long after our minds have forgotten the images of who we are. We come from God and we belong to Destiny; yet for some reason of ignorance we think that to be the master of our own fates and the captain of our own souls means to write everything down on a paper and plan everything out on a grid! Such great things to be done, and we think they are accomplished by our primitive ways! No. We must only know what we want. And want what we want. And then fly high enough to see all that which we want that we once could not yet see.

One of the most beneficial and valuable gifts we can give to ourselves in this life: is allowing ourselves to be surprised! It is okay if life surprises you. It's a good thing!

If you follow the ancient maps written on the stars, no person will ever understand you. So if you could read these maps, would you follow them? And forever be misunderstood? Or would you close your eyes tightly and pretend to be like everyone else?

Let go of the mistakes and the sins of others. You'll have plenty of time to make your own mistakes, the rest of your life to commit your own sins.

There is something simply beautiful and simply innocent— in being human. It is just so innocent and beautiful. I love it.

If you wait for a cake to be given to you so you will be happy, then you will be happy when someone gives you a cake. But if you buy a cake (or bake one) for yourself so you will be happy— you have found the way of happiness!

To buy a cake... to howl at the moon... to know true happiness... I am happy.

I don't define lust as anything evil or nasty. Lust as defined by me, is the feeling of desire: a desire to eat cake, a desire to feel the touch of another's skin moving over your own skin, a desire to breathe, a desire to live, a desire to laugh intensely like it was the best thing God ever created... this is lust as defined by me. And I think that's what it really is.

Such is my relationship with God: on my gigantic canvas of life, I am the one throwing all of the brightly-colored paints, creating genuine splatters, authentic whirlpools of color, beautiful patterns, wonderful streaks, stains and wild accents! God is the one with the paintbrush who stands beside my canvas, filling all the intricate and amazing details in-between the whirlpools and the streaks! We're happy together!

The only people for me are the ones who spill things, the ones who drop their cups sometimes, the ones who get dirty hands and messy hair, the ones who can go barefoot if they feel like it, the people who forget things, and can laugh at themselves every day...

Living is about capturing the essence of things. I go through my life every day with a vial: a vial wherein can be found precious essential oils of every kind! The priceless, fragrant oils that are the essence of my experiences, my thoughts. I walk inside a different realm from everybody else, in that I exist in the essence of things. Every time there is reason to smile, I hold out my glass vial and capture that drop of oil— that essence— and then I smile. And that is why I have smiled, and so you and I may be smiling at the same time but I am smiling because of that one drop of cherished, treasured oil that I have extracted. When I write I find no need to memorize an idea, a plot, a sequence of things, no. I must only capture the essence of a feeling or a thought and once I have inhaled that aroma, I know that I have what I need.

Peace is something like happiness; you cannot say, "I will be happy when..." and you can't say, "I will be peaceful when..." Your happiness shouldn't depend on the situation you're in nor on the circumstances that surround you. In the same breath, you cannot wait for everything around you to become peaceful in order for you to say, "I am

peaceful." In both happiness and peace, there is a heart of strength, determination and steadfastness. A heart that has the power to make things happen. You have to be at peace. You have to be happy.
Now.

Again, I am surprised why people seek to eliminate lust and cling to love as they wish to ignore happiness and cleave unto joy! Now, now, let's not sugarcoat things! Lust has a lot more to do with life and what is the good of life if you do not carry much lust inside of you at all times? And joy is a noble thing, but happiness though fleeting can be found every day and in every small little way!

Do not limit yourself to your own preconceptions of yourself, but throw yourself out onto a blank page that you haven't written on yet, and see what you find out about you, see what story unfolds, see what happens! I often do this and sometimes it can be very frightening: to often have a blank page with nothing written on it yet! I feel as though I am a soul with a single covering— my body of skin— and that's the only thing between me on the inside and the rest of the world! It's quite frightening to begin each day on a blank page, forgetting your own preconceptions of yourself and allowing your mind to embrace the new! It is like meeting yourself for the first time, over and over again!

We must not be defined by what we do, but we must be what and who we are; then only happen to do what we do!

The thing about traveling alone is that you run into your insecurities and fears times ten the normal! You run into all the good things and all the bad things about yourself on a daily basis, and are allowed the opportunity to truly become your own friend. Traveling alone is a learning process; some people travel for leisure, but I travel to run into myself!

I looked long and hard for the paper roses! I found the reddest red ribbon and a little golden card! We were all there together, many of us, in the same place; but I was the only one who found the paper roses, the only one who chose the reddest red ribbon and the only one who topped off with a golden card. And so I learned that if people are unhappy, it is sometimes because they don't know how to look for the paper roses, they don't see the reddest red ribbon and they don't like the little golden cards. We are all in the same wrap-shoppe in this life. But we are different. Because some of us are looking for the paper roses, choosing the reddest red ribbon and picking up the little golden cards.

Many things that don't really mean so much of anything, are wonderful.

I swear, the best things come to me by accident! Or should I say, effortless destiny?

Let us each take up our flaming torches and mount as the blazing fireballs of light that we are and let's burn the skies and leave it with deep scars and let them be our signatures upon eternity as we go forth!

...No— but ours is a journey into ourselves, a walk with God every day! Ours is a book that we write, a smile, a love, a tear, a lust, an awakening, a learning, a joy, a laughter, a memory, a dream, a vision, a love, a love, a love and a love. Our life is now. And Heaven is always there; but this life isn't always there, but this life isn't always here. Heaven is always there for us but this life is a gift to us!

Heaven is always there for us; but this life... this life is a gift to us.

Life is short and that's why, I don't test people; because we all fail tests sometimes, but that is supposed to be okay! I don't play games with people because people aren't toys. And I don't risk what I don't want to lose because if I do lose it, it's definitely my loss and not theirs! How short is life, you ask me. Well, life is as short as one drop in eternity. I swim in a single drop in this basin of eternal waters and after that drop evaporates, it's gone! But then you could argue that if life is just a drop then why even bother? Well, yes it is a drop, but it's a meaningful drop, an unforgettable drop and a beautiful one! It's so unforgettable, that when you come back again, if you choose to, you will remember it in your dreams at night! So you see, I don't test people, I don't play games and I don't risk who and what I don't want to lose.

Life is still better than University. In school, your teacher is the fruit picker and you are the open fruit basket. Then you take those fruits and make cakes and pies. But Life is going to give you the chance to go out there and pick those fruits yourself. Then you can eat them, or make them into something else, any which way— your own hands picked them!

Yes, you may have your cake and eat it too. I will only take the rest of the world along with all the other cakes in it, thank you!

All I really, really want to do is find a very, very fine chocolate store that I can walk into and then figure out how in the world one manages to pick out just a few chocolates out of all those very many chocolates! If I am one day able to walk into a fine chocolate store and know for certain which chocolates I want, when that happens, I will believe myself to be accomplished!

You just go a little crazy, you know. Sometimes. And why? Well only because your soul is just too big for you, it flies away somehow.

I think that there are those who write of life being a skip on the sidewalk, a chocolate bar, a bowl of cherries... the problem with that is it ends up disappointing people. Because life is more like being on the tube in London: you never really know what could happen! But then there are those people who bring a box of chocolates to eat on the tube... so life— it isn't a skip on the sidewalk, but it is a matter of strength: "Can I bring my bowl of cherries to feast on while I stand here in the gutter?" that's the essence of life. Can you still put on your rose-colored glasses while your eyes are filled with tears and see everything in rosy colors? That's the strength that fuels a true life. Can you think to bring your little box of chocolates with you while you sit on the tube running under the streets of London? Because you should. Because even if you don't know anybody and you don't know what's going to happen next, you should still have your box of chocolates with you. You should eat your bowl of cherries. And that is what life is.

The knowledge of secrets is a very enticing ship, a very tempting voyage and one thinks that the highest attainment in life is to find out hidden truths, to seek out what is truth, to know what are all lies: to uncover, to discover and to rediscover, to dig up, to expose, to reveal... But secrets can go on forever, for an eternity! For as vast as the universe is— so are the secrets therein! And one can lose, because of that thought that in the secrets, everything is to be gained! But I can see, that all the knowledge of hidden things, all the knowledge in the universe, is not nearly as valuable and as worthy as the innocence of one's soul. And we are not directed unto good things through our ability to scavenge or to hunt or to decipher or to sail! Or to fly! But we are directed unto good things, through Sovereign Providence! He is more worthy— the innocent soul who has a simple faith in what he believes in— than the one who has found out all the dark secrets about what the other man has put his faith in! And it is far more profitable for a man to be healthy, to have a long, long life, loved ones that are blessed with these blessings all the same, much love and happiness and safety! It is far more profitable for a man to be able to remain innocent and have love and be healthy and to be able to watch his loved ones in good health and in good love, than for a man to uncover all the secrets of the universe! A single love, a single faith, a single trust, and one hope— these are far, far better things to aspire to have! And this— this is the biggest secret!

"Do you have a leather jacket? One for a ten-year-old boy?" I asked the man selling leather jackets and gloves in Covent Garden, London. "Yes, I have one right here!" And the man dug out a fine leather jacket that looked styled and tailored for a young boy. "I'm buying this for my son" I said to him. "I love this jacket, it's perfect, I think I will just come back for it tomorrow, though! I'll be back tomorrow, okay?" And the man reached his arms above his head and said with a big smile upon his face "You only have one life to live! What is the difference if you do something today, or if you do it tomorrow?" I thought about the man's words. And I bought the jacket. He was right, there is no difference, really, between doing something today and doing something tomorrow when you only have one life to live! After all, tomorrow may never come! All you really have is today!

What if... all the rules and ways we lay down in our heads, don't even exist at all? What if we only believe that they're there, because we want to think that they're there? All the formalities of morality and the decisions that we see ourselves making in order to be better (or the best)... what if we think we've got it all under control, but we don't? What if the path for you, is one that you would never dare take because you never saw yourself going that way? And then what if you realized that, one day? Would you take the path for you? Or would you choose to believe in your rules and your reasons? Your moralities and your hopes? What if your own hope and your own morality— are going the other way?

times you just don't know what's ng to happen, exactly. And that's because sometimes you just don't have control over circumstances in your life. The amazing thing is that— it is during these times that we free-fall through the sky! All we have is the breath in our lungs right here and right now and it's just exhilarating! And it takes humility to accept that we might not have everything we want in our hands at the moment— but that what we do have is good, is worth keeping. Even if something isn't everything yet, it can be worth everything, right now! You just have to spread your arms in the air and start gliding!

People have this dream of being unreachable. They build a name for themselves and then finally fulfill their dream of "being more important."

Which just shows they were born from down below. Because when you're born from up above, your dreams have nowhere to go but downwards! And you dream of doing things in order to meet people, to know them, to understand the smallest importances!

Lots of people are born into lives that feel like a journey in the very middle of a big ship on familiar seas: they sit comfortably, crossing their legs, they know when the sun will rise and when the moon will wane, they have plans that they follow, they have a map! But then there are those of us, a few, who are born into lives that feel like standing at the very top of the ship's stern: we have to stand up, hold on tight for dear life, we never know when the waves will rock and we never know where the sun will set or when the moon will wane!

Nothing follows the laws of common nature and we live in a wild, wild awakening and the only map we have is the map of the stars! We're called to see the lightning tear at the horizon, we're chosen to roar with the tempests, but we're also the first ones to see the suns rise, the first ones to watch the moons form anew! There is nothing ordinary, nothing at all. But neither are we! And we wouldn't want it any other way!

All sorrows in life stem from the lack of cake. If you had your own cake, you wouldn't bother trying to take away the other person's cake! And, if the cake you had were beautiful enough, you wouldn't bother trying to melt the icing on that other person's cake! And if you always had a very beautiful cake that was always beautiful enough, then you would have a smile on your face all the time and wouldn't even care if other people were enjoying their own cakes! Because you'd be enjoying yours, too! Therefore, I hereby decree that all sorrows can be fixed by many beautiful cakes. Bake a cake!

Travel is the best teacher. The only way to an open mind is by taking a plane out into the open world.

Eleutheromania

(n.) A manic or frantic desire for freedom.

Sometimes I just stand there under the sky and look up and say, "Please, please, anywhere but here, please." And it's in those moments that I believe that I, too, deserve freedom. I deserve to feel free.

Life is too short to waste any amount of time on wondering what other people think about you. In the first place, if they had better things going on in their lives, they wouldn't have the time to sit around and talk about you. What's important to me is not others' opinions of me, but what's important to me is my opinion of myself.

For too long now, I have not let myself be myself. But now... I am going to let myself be me.

Pain is a pesky part of being human, I've learned it feels like a stab wound to the heart, something I wish we could all do without, in our lives here. Pain is a sudden hurt that can't be escaped. But then I have also learned that because of pain, I can feel the beauty, tenderness and freedom of healing. Pain feels like a fast stab wound to the heart. But then healing feels like the wind against your face when you are spreading your wings and flying through the air! We may not have wings growing out of our backs; but healing is the closest thing that will give us that wind against our faces.

"They are angry with me, because I know what I am." Said the little eagle.

"How do you know that they are angry with you?" Asked the wise old owl.

"Because, they despise me for wanting to soar, they only want me to peck at the dirt, looking for ants with them. But I can't do that. I don't have chicken feet, I have eagle wings!"

"And what is so wrong with having eagle wings and no chicken feet?" Asked the old owl.

"I'm not sure, that's what I'm trying to find out."

"They hate you because you know that you are an eagle and they want you to think you are a chicken so that you will peck at the ground looking for ants and worms, so that you will never know that you are an eagle and always think yourself a chicken. Let them hate you, they will always be chickens, and you will always be an eagle! You must fly. You must soar!" Said the wise old owl.

~ Full parable found in *The Sun Is Snowing: Poems, Parables and Pictures*

I think that if you have a horse, pegasus, qilin, or unicorn— you should sit on it! You should stroke its hair, whisper in its ear, be one with it! And you shouldn't feel sorry if other people don't have one.

The unhappiest people in this world are those who care the most about what other people think.

People have to forgive. We don't have to like them, we don't have to be friends with them, we don't have to send them hearts in text messages, but we have to forgive them, to overlook, to forget. Because if we don't we are tying rocks to our feet, too much for our wings to carry!

You will find that it is necessary to let things go simply for the reason that they are heavy. So let them go, let go of them. I tie no weights to my ankles!

I wish that the world were just one big place, that there were no borders, no lines, no fences and no gates. I wish that people weren't so far away and that if you wanted to be near someone— you just could. I wish the world were that simple. It should be that simple. That's the way it should be.

If you want to forget something or someone, never hate it, or never hate him/her. Everything and everyone that you hate is engraved upon your heart; if you want to let go of something, if you want to forget; you cannot hate.

When I was a little girl, everything in the world fell into either of these two categories: wrong or right, black or white. Now that I am an adult, I have put childish things aside and now I know that some things fall into wrong and some things fall into right. Some things are categorized as black and some things are categorized as white. But most things in the world aren't either! Most things in the world aren't black, aren't white, aren't wrong, aren't right; but most of everything is just different. And now I know that there's nothing wrong with different and that we can let things be different, we don't have to try and make them black or white, we can just let them be grey. And when I was a child, I thought that God was the God who only saw black and white. Now that I am no longer a child, I can see, that God is the God who can see the black and the white and the grey, too, and He dances on the grey! Grey is okay.

Lots of things can be fixed. Things can be fixed. But many times, relationships between people cannot be fixed, because they should not be fixed. You're aboard a ship setting sail, and the other person has joined the inland circus, or is boarding a different ship and you just can't be with each other anymore. Because you shouldn't be.

Last night I lost the world, and gained the universe.

Don't think about making life better for other people who don't even deserve you, rather, focus on making your life the best, for yourself and those who love you.

No, I am not bitter, I am not hateful and I am not unforgiving. I just don't like you.

Anger is like flowing water: there's nothing wrong with it as long as you let it flow. Hate is like stagnant water: anger that you denied yourself the freedom to feel, the freedom to flow, water that you gathered in one place and left to forget. Stagnant water becomes dirty, stinky, disease-ridden, poisonous, deadly: that is your hate. On flowing water travels little paper boats: paper boats of forgiveness. Allow yourself to feel anger, allow your waters to flow along with all the paper boats of forgiveness. Be human.

The day I understood everything was the day I stopped trying to figure everything out. The day I knew peace was the day I let everything go.

People wait around too long for love. I'm happy with all of my lusts!

Choose your battles wisely. After all, life isn't measured by how many times you stood up to fight. It's not winning battles that makes you happy, but it's how many times you turned away and chose to look into a better direction! Life is too short to spend it on warring. Fight only the most, most, most important ones, let the rest go!

Never do a single thing in the anticipation to prove something to someone who has hurt you. If someone has hurt or offended you (whoever that person may be), never perform anything or strive for anything in your life with the mind of proving something to that someone/ to those people. May nothing that you do be done with any thought of them in mind. There is nothing that needs to be proven.

There came a time in my life, when, cornered by so many detractors, I had to just say “So you like it when I’m cute, bashful and timid. And of course you like me that way because you can walk all over me that way. However, I really don’t feel cute, I’m not a fan of bashful and I don’t care for timidity. Actually my eyes are rather wild, my style rather confident and my approach very warm. So you will just have to not like me. The wonderful thing is that your not liking me makes no difference whatsoever in my life.” And when that epiphany happened— that’s when I finally began to breathe again. Said to myself “What the hell were you doing for so long, caring if people liked you for so long?” Besides, they always like you; they just can’t be you and that’s what they don’t like.

People can have their opinions about everything in the world, but people's opinions end where the tip of my nose begins. Your opinions of others can only go so far as to where their own shoreline is. The world is for your taking; but other people are not. One is only allowed to have an opinion of me, if that person is done educating him/herself on everything about me. Before people educate themselves on everything about you, they're not allowed to open their venomous mouths and have an opinion about you.

Anger is an essential part of being human. People are taught to deny themselves anger, and in this, they are actually opening themselves up to hate. The more you deny yourself the freedom to be angry, the more you will hate. Let yourself be angry and hate will disintegrate, and when hate disintegrates, forgiveness prevails! The more you deny that you are angry, in attempts to be "holy" the more inhuman you will become and the more inhuman you will become, the harder it will be to forgive.

"I don't look for love. Love looks for me."

"Why?"

"Because it needs me. Because I'm not afraid of it."

The majority of people have successfully alienated themselves from change. They tediously arrange their lives into a familiar pattern, they give themselves to normalcy, they are proud if they are able to follow in auspicious footsteps set before them, they take pride in always coloring inside the lines and they feel secure if they belong to a batch of others who are like them. Now, if familiar patterns bore you, if normalcy passes before you unnoticed, if you want to create your own footsteps in the earth and leave your own handprints on the skies, if you are the one who doesn't mind the lines in the coloring book as much as others do, and perchance you do not cling to a flock for you to identify with, then you must be ready for adversity! If you are something extraordinary, you are going to always shock others and while they go about existing in their mundaneness which they call success; you're going to be flying around crazy in their skies and that scares them. People are afraid of change, afraid of being different, afraid of doing things and thinking things that aren't a part of their checkerboard game of a life. They only know the pieces and the moves in their games, and that's it. You're always going to find them in the place that you think you're going to find them in, and every time they think about you— you're going to give them a heart attack.

I am not a little bit of many things; but I am the sufficient representation of many things. I am not an incompletion of all these races; but I am a masterpiece of the prolific. I am an entirety, I am not a lack of anything; rather, I am a whole of many things. God did not see it needful to make me generic. He thinks I am better than that.

I am always coming back to roses. I have tried having many different types of favorite flowers since I was told that the rose is "such a common" favorite flower to have. It made me feel bad and so I looked for another. At one time I chose the iris, another time I chose the orchid. At other times the jasmine or the water lily. But today I know for sure that my favorite flower is the rose and in all of her perfect colors! As long as she is a rose! Many flowers are beautiful; but the rose makes me feel that I am just where I am supposed to be, at any given moment in time! She surpasses time— she is eternity. She reminds me that I swim in eternity and that destiny is on my side. When I see a yellow rose, I see the favor of the gods upon me. When I see a pink rose, I feel like I'm home, while red roses are as untamed as my passions. And the blue rose... oh the blue rose that no words can describe! And so you see, I have decided that if people think I am common for loving the rose— then people are stupid.

Yesterday I was sad, today I am happy! Yesterday I had a problem; today I still have the same problem! But today I changed the way I look at it!

As you go about your daily life, you will encounter many lemons. Sour expressions, sour attitudes and sour auras! The good thing is that if you don't want to be a lemon, you don't have to be! Just don't let those lemons rub themselves all over you! And you don't even have to save them! Let lemons be lemons! One of the most important things that I have ever learned is that I don't have to save people.

I don't have a diary, I don't write things into a diary. I imprint myself into the sky and when the sunlight shines brightly, I can stand under the sun's rays and everything I have imprinted of myself into the sky I will begin to see again, feel again, remember. And when the wind begins to blow, it blows the details over my face, and I remember everything I left in the sky and see new things being born. I am unwritten.

Some people are like thorns. But you have to let them be thorns, because thorns can't turn into petals. The trick is not letting them prick you! Never let a thorn prick you!

The difference between me and other people is that they all walk around with onion skins wrapped around them. Premeditations, pretentions, the faces that they present to the world, the faces that they present to themselves... onionskins that come in layer after layer. They're on the inside of all that. And I... I am the inside of the onionskin walking around. I am only me.

It would be perfect if everyone who makes love were in love; but this is simply an unrealistic expectation. I'd say 75 percent of the population of people who make love, are not in love, this is simply the reality of the human race, and to be idealistic about this is to wait for the stars to align and Jupiter to change color, for the Heavens to etch your names together in the sky before you make love to someone. But idealism is immaturity and as a matter of fact, the stars may never align, Jupiter may never change color, and the Heavens may never ever etch your names together in the sky for you to have the never-ending permission to make endless love to one another! And so the bottom line is, there really is no difference between doing something today or doing something tomorrow, because today is what you have, and tomorrow may not turn out the way you expect it to. At the end of the day, sex is an animalistic, humanistic, passionate desire.

(Disclaimer: Written when jaded.)

Many times, you are the single most significant and glorious thing that has ever happened in the lives of some people, they sit around and talk about you over and over again throughout the years while you are out there living your ery step that you take and every kiss that you make having absolutely nothing to do with them, at all!

Some people live in cages with bars built from their own fears and doubts. Some people live in cages with bars built from other people's fears and doubts: their parents, their friends, their brothers and sisters, their families. Some people live in cages with bars built from the choices others made for them, the circumstances other people imposed upon them. And some people break free.

I find no importance in showing others that I am happy, it's not important to me that they know or think that I am happy but what is important to me is that I am happy. I am interested in *being* happy; not in making others think or know that I am.

You can have a pet zebra and put that zebra into a small cage every day and tell the zebra that you love it but no matter how you and the zebra love each other; the fact remains, that the zebra should be let out of that cage and should belong to someone who can treat it better, the way it should be treated, someone who can make it happy.

Man is not defiled by his impurities. It is the other man pointing out his impurities to him, whom he is defiled by. Is there anything anyone can do, to become righteous, anyway? God made us impure. If he had a problem with that, He would have made us gods, instead.

I don't understand why people care so much about showing that they are good, because I am rather comfortable with having badness, quite okay with being inexplicable. They tire themselves so. The light is beautiful; but light can't hide treasures like the darkness can.

She had a flower tattoo on her wrist... "What does that mean?" he asked her. "Absolutely nothing," she said, "it's just a flower."

Please do not break your heart ov withering of a dream you once held that never became yours! After all, the shattered dream could have very well been a nightmare and not a dream at all, you wouldn't really know because you didn't have it yet! Let the sparks fade, let the flame dim and die, you'll never know it wasn't poison.

"I have just lost my reason for fighting so hard. How do I go on now, without my thing to fight for?" And he whispered into my ear, he said: "Maybe it's time to stop fighting."

Our parents can show us a lot of things: they can show us how we are to be and what things we ought to strive for or they can show us how not to be and what things we ought to stray from, then you may have the kind of parents that show you all the things about you that you want to get rid of and you realize those traits aren't yours at all but are merely your parents' marks that have rubbed off onto you.

There's that "margin of error" that you allow to exist in your mind, you want to give everything the benefit of the doubt, you want to look at another person and say "maybe we could be friends" and that's all well at first, but then you have to reach that point in your life wherein you don't have time to live on the margins of error and you have to say, "So what if there is a margin of error that exists? I don't think that this person and I could walk down the same path together, because she's like that, and I'm like this! I must relieve myself of fearing

the error, the 'what could have been'."
You know, sometimes we can be so afraid of *the what could have been* that we overlook *the right here and now!* We end up forsaking who we are and what makes us happy and what we want and don't want! There is an error that takes place when living too much for *the what could have been*. There comes a time when you must give *yourself* the benefit of the doubt! Know thyself. Color-in those margins of error with your favorite color, make them your own, make them work for you, let them be in your favor!

It's neither the law of religion nor the principles of morality that define our highways and pathways to God; only by the Grace of God are we led and drawn, to God. It is His grace that conquers a multitude of flaws and in that grace there is only favor. Favor is not achieved; favor is received.

If anything or anyone removes peace from you or inflicts confusion and judgment on you, this thing or person is not of God regardless of whether or not that person or thing has wrapped itself/himself in the wrapping paper with God's face printed all over it. Don't stop believing in God but stop believing in that person, in that thing. The wrapping paper with God's face stamped all over it isn't really God.

"I don't ask people to keep me."

~ *Lucy Toscana Nightingberg,* from the novella *Saint Paul Trois Châteaux: 1948*

Today I am someone different. Today I have finally become who I really am.

Life is not compassionate towards victims. The trick is not to see yourself as one. It's never too late! I know I've felt like the victim in various situations in my life, but, it's never too late for me to realize that it's my responsibility to stand on victorious ground and know that whatever it is I'm experiencing or going through— those are just the clouds rolling by while I stand here on the top of this mountain! This mountain called Victory! The clouds will come and the clouds will go, but the truth is that I'm high up here on this mountaintop that reaches into the sky! I am a victor. I didn't climb up the mountain; I was born on top of it!

A concerned churchgoer asked me: "Is your relationship with God okay?" and I answered, "My relationship with God is far better than yours. You have to be in a certain place, with a certain group of people, pray at certain days of the week, read the Bible at certain times of the day— all in order to have a relationship with God. But I am with God from the moment I wake up, to the moment I fall asleep at night, I am with God wherever on this earth that I wander to and whosoever I may be with! I may be sitting on the subway, and I am with God. I can assure you that I am closer to God than you are."

It's time that I stop referring to myself, thinking about myself, planning for myself, according to the gridlines and the timelines and the guidelines of people. I will expand in this universe; I will not stay on the lines or within the lines written by this world.

I am a siren and for my adoration of mankind, have been caught in fishing nets one time too many. And in those fishing nets I have learned too many unfavorable things about human intentions and the lack of trust and goodwill. So I'm not going to allow myself to be caught, anymore. Sirens do well at singing the sirens' song and dragging vile people to their deaths, and for good reason!

Freedom is not the absence of commitment, and to be committed to something or to someone does not mean the loss of freedom. But freedom exists in the realm of the unbound and to be free is to be committed to that which is a part of the unbound realm. Whatever sets your soul to flight is freedom. If someone sets your soul to flight, to stay with that person is not to lose freedom but to stay with that person is to retain freedom. Together you have what is unbound. Whatever will swell your spirit and give you wings, is freedom, and it is a fault if you let go of that for the very reason that you are afraid of losing it, and in doing so you have in fact let go of what will keep you unbound.

Love is a devoted madness while marriage is a responsibility. But then it is possible to be devotedly mad and responsible at the same time, yes it is. And so this is how we should begin to see marriage: as it is, for what it is! Marriage needs to cease being an eternal ideal with the predestined ending of death! We must allow it to be and to appear as what it is! Perhaps if we approach marriage with eyes open to the reality of the nature of it, we will stop failing at it! We fail at it because we think of it as something it is not! We are romanced by an ideal that is not in touch with reality and that's why when we begin to discover the reality of it, we see ourselves as failures! It is a wild and blessed thing to want to spend the rest of your adult life with one person, growing and changing together, while stepping deeper into the depths of love; notwithstanding, we must understand that we may not get it "right" the first time.

Freedom is a place, an area. It's a higher place. There are some other people that are here and things that are here, which are unseen. But you first have to set yourself free and believe in what you cannot see, believe that there is something more out there. In freedom can be found many devotions: a devotion to love, a desire to believe, a willingness to be happy, a perseverance to have peace. All these unseen things breathe and grow in the unseen soul. A free person is not an uncommitted person; but in a free person you will find a deep devotion and a desire to be devoted to even more.

I found goodness in the place that I once believed to be evil and found evil in the place that I once always believed to be good! The truth is so far separated from where I thought it existed. It can be such a wild, unbound journey: the journey from the illusion into the truth. Some people take that journey; but more people don't.

Love is greater than marriage; love is the greater thing while marriage, though noble and honorable, is questionable in its origins. I question the creations of man; I do not question the masterpieces of God.

In all things in this life, we are told "It's okay if you don't make it the first time!", "It's fine if you don't get it right the first time, just try again and again!" We are told this in learning how to ride a bike, in learning how to bake a cake, in solving our math equations... in everything. Except marriage. Why are we all expected to get such an enormous and weighty thing right, the very first time and if we don't we're considered as failures? I beg to differ! That is a stupidity!

And that's when I heard the whisper in my heart's ear: "It's not about your childhood. It's about who you are!"

Previously, as I went through life, I was in full belief of the concept of "blending" (I was fully convinced that I, as a person, am completely capable of blending myself in the accordance of friendship, in order to give respect to the differences between people and in order for others to feel that I respect them). However, I have come to learn at this time in my life, that such an attitude is all good for a while; but then there does come a point where you must see and identify yourself, also see and identify others! You have to be able to identify yourself as someone who is made happy by this and as someone who doesn't like that, then when you meet people, discern if those same things are the things that make them happy and if those same things are the things that they don't like. Because at a point in time it becomes beneficial to you, to not waste time on blending in behalf of virtue but rather it becomes beneficial to you, to see yourself and go into the direction that makes you happy, taking people with you that are already going in that same direction and who also do not like the things that you do not like. At the end of the day, there are those paths in life and you have to take one of them; you can't walk down all of them.

We are all tricked. We think that religion tells us what to believe; but it doesn't, it is telling us what not to believe. Atheism is not the absence of religion; atheism is the most undiluted form of religion: it tells us not to believe in anything at all. Atheists hate the religious and the religious hate atheists, but this is only a deception! We are all deceived! There is only one boat and we are all in it! All at the same time!

Anybody who says, "I know how to get to God and you don't, so do this and do that and go here and go there" is going to become 1. Very powerful, and 2. Very rich. The simple truth is that if I am with God, no less can you be with God at the same time as I am.

I believe that the heartbeat of God can be felt in everything. The concept of God is not aloof to me, nor is it difficult for me to grasp! When I see the tender embrace of a father— I see God. When I breathe— I breathe God, He moves inside my lungs! I am not without God, because God is in everything!

No more quickly can a person rob you of your joy and peace than when that individual succeeds at making you feel like you're less than worthy of God as compared to his/her own self. The old adage "You're on your way to hell and I'm on my way to heaven" spoken or implied to another, is the most predominantly effective way to make someone feel better about himself, and he doesn't even have to prove that he is better in this life on earth because now he can just say "Wait 'til I'm looking down at you while you're in hell!" But please don't be robbed of your joy and peace because individuals or groups of people like that don't know where God is. He is a whisper-distance away from you, is all.

If you ask the religious person "What do you believe in?" he will tell you about one thing. But if you ask him "What do you not believe in?" he will tell you about many, many things! And if you ask an atheist "What do you believe in?" that atheist will say "Nothing." The only difference between an atheist and a religious person is one thing. If the one thing weren't there, there would be no difference at all! When I say I am losing my religion, I am not saying that I'm losing my belief; but I am saying that I'm losing my disbeliefs.

There are gigantic trees that have grown tall into the winds and the clouds over the thousands of years of their lives, their tops are rustled and tossed by the mists of the atmosphere! Then there are the short trees that don't live for long, they are young with no deep roots and only a few annual rings to tell their stories. The tall, ancient trees sway in the realm of freedom while the short young trees cannot even raise their branches into that direction of the sky! Now, you are the bird who needs a tree to live in; if you choose to live in the tree, which thrives in the realm of freedom, that doesn't mean you are not committed to that tree. You are still committed to your tree, but together you and your tree live in freedom.

Freedom is not the absence of commitment. If you are the bird who chooses to fly around amongst the short trees and live in them, that's because your wings are too short to make it any higher and your vision too near to see any further into the clouds. And if you move from one short tree to the next short tree, that doesn't mean you are free, you are still down there below, freedom is still nowhere near you.

Wanna know the fastest way to unhappiness? Spend your time judging other people's reasons for happiness! That way, you'll quickly lose your own! The next time you look back at yourself (when you've taken a break from judging others) you'll think "Oh! Where did *my* happiness go?" because you were too busy thinking that gay people shouldn't be happy... or, you know, something like that.

That day, they jumped into the river together. It was hot and nobody needed any clothes.

~ *Saint Paul Trois Châteaux: 1948*

Our relationship with God is not about doing right and not doing wrong; but it's simply about walking on this earth with the same One whom we walked with before we came to this earth! It's a continuum. It is, in itself, a part of *aeternum!*

If you buy an egg thinking it's a goose's egg, and when it hatches it is actually a bird of paradise; no manner of convincing and reproach will turn the bird of paradise into a goose. Even if you make it go to goose church and goose school and eat goose feeds and only hang out with geese! In the end, it will still belong to paradise.

People create sins out of nothing and in doing so have enslaved their fellow man! Man is not bound by sin but man is bound by the idea that almost everything he is doing is a sin!

If you lack the humility to go back and tie up the loose ends in your past, then be prepared to forever be haunted by her ghosts, all of whom will come into your present and your future— staining everything and everyone with their leftover emotional and mental garbage.

Humility is the master key that can get you out of all your cages; why do you choose your ego and stay in your prisons?

Eros (or call it lust if you will) is like a beautiful, magnificent Afghan hound! A pure white Afghan hound commanding respect and honor! But if you take the Afghan hound and lock it in a small cage, shun it and look upon it badly, treat it as a pestilence and wish that it would die, that same creature of beauty will become a vile, unrepentant, dark creature of the shadows! Untrusting, hidden in the corner, aggressive... something that will harm others and yourself! But is this the nature of the creature, is this the fault of the creature? Or are *you* the one who has created the monster that it has become? This is my philosophy: that we are both corporeal and incorporeal beings, therefore, the same amount of good intent *must* be given to both our soul and our body!

Eudaimonia

(n.) From "eu" (good) and "daemon" (spirit), is a central concept in Aristotelian ethics and is best translated as "human flourishing"; the "highest human good"

Truth was a colored glass window that God dropped to the earth. Truth shattered into many colorful pieces and some of those pieces lay on mountaintops, some on seashores, some in the oceans and others on the rocks... each of these pieces of glass was found by someone, and every one of those people, so taken in by the beauty of the thing, declared it the one-and-only truth in the universe! And so it happens that everyone has a part of the whole colored glass window that shattered on the earth; but instead of looking for all the other parts of it; they hold onto their one discovery, shunning all the other ones because they are of different colors. And I sit here and I think as I look upon them and I say to myself, *if only they would come together and put all the pieces of the window together, they would see that it would be something so beautiful...*

We have to allow ourselves to be loved by the people who really love us, the people who really matter. Too much of the time, we are blinded by our own pursuits of people to love us, people that don't even matter, while all that time we waste and the people who do love us have to stand on the sidewalk and watch us beg in the streets! It's time to put an end to this. It's time for us to let ourselves be loved.

There is no such thing as a "broken family." Family is family and is not determined by marriage certificates, divorce papers and adoption documents. Families are made in the heart. The only time family becomes null is when those ties in the heart are cut. If you cut those ties, those people are not your family. If you make those ties, those people are your family. And if you hate those ties, those people will still be your family because whatever you hate will always be with you.

What is life if it is only lived by what one perceives to be reality? When it is the things that seem to be unreal that are worth living for! What's the reason for life, if there are no surprises, no people and moments that catch you unawares and sweep you off of your feet? Aaahhh... but we live for all things that seem to be unreal... and we long to find them.

The only person who can pull me down is myself, and I'm not going to let myself pull me down anymore.

The ego is like a coffin that the human soul resides in whilst the body is still alive! It inhibits the soul from having vision and from seeing beyond, from experiencing the world in its full beauty and potential, from letting people in and bringing people out, from growing and breathing and becoming something more! The ego quite literally acts as a soul's coffin! And it is the most unfortunate thing for one to live one's entire life, inside of it! Ego is to the human soul, what disease is to the human body!

In our lives, we will always meet those who are greater than ourselves and those who are lesser than ourselves. It is not for us to pull down the greater and it is not for us to demean the lesser. But it is for us to pull up the lesser and learn from the greater. They key to this is to always know where we are. If the greater reaches out, we should learn. If the lesser seeks shade, we should spread our wings.

I think the truth is that, you really can't whore yourself to people. You can give people your very best intentions, your very best sincerities; and they can take that and spit on it. And you feel bad because you couldn't be loved in return. The trick is to realize that you weren't meant to be loved by people who don't know what diamonds are; you were meant to be loved by those who appreciate the diamond and all cuts and shapes and colors. And there are stones available for those who want stones, so don't worry about the stone-lovers. To each his own.

There is some kind of a sweet innocence in being human— in not having to be just happy or just sad— in the nature of being able to be both broken and whole, at the same time.

I think that we are like stars. Something happens to burst us open; but when we burst open and think we are dying; we're actually turning into a supernova. And then when we look at ourselves again, we see that we're suddenly more beautiful than we ever were before!

You can be the most beautiful person in the world and everybody sees light and rainbows when they look at you, but if you yourself don't know it, all of that doesn't even matter. Every second that you spend on doubting your worth, every moment that you use to criticize yourself, is a second of your life wasted, is a moment of your life thrown away. It's not like you have forever, so don't waste any of your seconds, don't throw even one of your moments away.

Don't think about making life better for other people who don't even deserve you, rather, focus on making your life the best, for yourself and those who love you.

I am my own biggest critic. Before anyone else has criticized me, I have already criticized myself. But for the rest of my life, I am going to be with me and I don't want to spend my life with someone who is always critical. So I am going to stop being my own critic. It's high time that I accept all the great things about me.

The person in life that you will always be with the most is yourself. Because even when you are with others, you are still with yourself, too! When you wake up in the morning, you are with yourself, lying in bed at night you are with yourself, walking down the street in the sunlight you are with yourself. What kind of person do you want to walk down the street with? What kind of ıon do you want to wake up in the morning with? What kind of person do you want to see at the end of the day before you fall asleep? Because that person is yourself and it's your responsibility to be that person you want to be with. I know I want to spend my life with a person who knows how to let things go, who's not full of hate, who's able to smile and be carefree. So that's who I have to be.

You're going to meet many people with domineering personalities: the loud, the obnoxious, those that noisily stake their claims in your territory and everywhere else they set foot on. This is the blueprint of a predator. Predators prey on gentleness, peace, calmness, sweetness and any positivity that they sniff out as weakness. Anything that is happy and at peace they mistake for weakness. It's not your job to change these people; but it's your job to show them that your peace and gentleness do not equate to weakness. I have always appeared to be fragile and delicate but the thing is— I am not fragile and I am not delicate. I am very gentle but I can show you that the gentle also possess a poison. I compare myself to silk. People mistake silk to be weak but a silk handkerchief can protect the wearer from a gunshot. There are many people who will want to befriend you if you fit the description of what they think is weak: predators want to have friends that they can dominate over because that makes them feel strong and important. The truth is that predators have no strength and no courage. It is you who are strong and it is you who has courage. I have lost many a friend over the fact that when they attempt to rip me— they can't! They accuse me of being deceiving; I am not deceiving, I am just made of silk. It is they who are stupid and wrongly take gentleness and fairness for weakness. There are many more predators in this world, so I want you to be made of silk. You are silk.

I am a flawed person. A brook with many stones, a clear blue sky with many blackbirds. I have many shortcomings. A rainbow that's not long enough, a starry night with clouds. But I can only be thankful to the God who loves me just this way and I can only be grateful to the people in my life who accept the clear blue sky with many blackbirds and who are patient with the rainbow that isn't long enough. And because of this, I am taught love, because of this I love my God and I love these people.

For everything in this journey of life we are on, there is a right wing and a left wing: for the wing of love there is anger; for the wing of destiny there is fear; for the wing of pain there is healing; for the wing of hurt there is forgiveness; for the wing of pride there is humility; for the wing of giving there is taking; for the wing of tears there is joy; for the wing of rejection there is acceptance; for the wing of judgment there is grace; for the wing of honor there is shame; for the wing of letting go there is the wing of keeping. We can only fly with two wings and two wings can only stay in the air if there is a balance. Two beautiful wings is perfection. There is a generation of people who idealize perfection as the existence of only one of these wings every time. But I see that a bird with one wing is imperfect. An angel with one wing is imperfect. A butterfly with one wing is dead. So this generation of people strives to always cut off the other wing in the hopes of embodying their ideal of perfection and in doing so, have created a crippled race.

I find it odd— the greed of mankind. People only like you for as long as they perceive they can get what they want from you. Or for as long as they perceive you are who they want you to be. But I like people for all of their changing surprises, the thoughts in their heads, the warmth that changes to cold and the cold that changes to warmth... for being human. The rawness of being human delights me.

The most adventurous journey to embark on: is the journey to yourself, ost exciting thing to discover: is ou really are, the most treasured es that you can find: are all the pieces of you, the most special portrait you can recognize: is the portrait of your soul.

I know from the bottom of my heart and with all of it, that it doesn't matter if at the end of your life you can say that you shared the best of yourself with the rest of the world and it doesn't matter if everyone in the world remembers you as wonderful; but what matters is if at the end of your life you can say that you shared the best of yourself with the handful of people who are around you, that you gave the wonderful in you to the people you love and who love you. Happiness never has, and never will come from fame.

The downfall of the attempts of governments and leaders to unite mankind is found in this: in the wrong message that we should see everyone as the same. This is the root of the failure of harmony. Because the truth is, we should not all see everyone as the same! We are not the same! We are made of different colours and we have different cultures. We are all different! But the key to this door is to look at these differences, respect these differences, learn from and about these differences and grow in and with these differences. We are all different. We are not the same. But that's beautiful. And that's okay. In the quest for unity and peace, we cannot blind ourselves and expect to be all the same. Because in this, we all have an underlying belief that everyone should be the same as us at some point. W[illegible] not on a journey to become the [illegible] to be the same. But we are on a [illegible]ney to see that in all of our [illegible]nces— that is what makes us beautiful as a human race and if we are ever to grow, we ought to learn and always learn some more.

It is when we think we can act like God, that all respect is lost and I think this is the downfall of peace. We lie if we say we do not see colour and culture and difference. We fool ourselves and cheat ourselves when we say that all of us are the same. We should not want to be the same as others and we should not want others to be the same as us. Rather, we ought to glory and shine in all of our differences, flaunting them fabulously for all to see! It is never a conformity that we need! We need not to conform! What we need is to burst out into all these beautiful colors!

people come and go and are ...gotten. But there are other people who share a part in our destinies. They come, they go, but they are never forgotten. They come, they go, but even after they go... they're still here. They never really went anywhere.

My spirit is healthy, yes. But I tell you, my flesh is healthy too. I am enlightened and free, but I am also lustful and carnal.

It is when you lose sight of yourself, that you lose your way. To keep your truth in sight you must keep yourself in ... d the world to you should be a ... reflect to you your image, the ... should be a mirror that you reflect upon.

I am never alone wherever I am. The air itself supplies me with a century of love. When I breathe in: I am breathing in the laughter, tears, victories, passions, thoughts, memories, existence, joys, moments and the hues of the sunlight on many tones of skin, I am breathing in the same air that was exhaled by many before me. The air that bore them life. And so how can I ever say that I am alone?

I think that the best kind of change is the change that comes from the inside and begins it's way out until it emerges on the outside: a change that is born underneath then continues and spread until it has reached the surface! true change. A powerful change have found that while we are emerging, transforming into something glorious: it is actually us becoming who we really are! A water lily is born underneath the water, inside the soil at the bottom of the river or lake. The water lily has *always been* a water lily for that whole time that it was sprouting out of the wet soil, reaching up through the dark water towards the sunlight, stretching and grasping for the surface where it then buds and blooms on the top, in the sunshine; it doesn't bud and bloom on the surface where all the light and the glory is and then try to reach down below into the soil. But it keeps its color all throughout its journey to emergence! It stays true to its lily nature so when it has reached full ascension on the top of the water— it is not a tulip, a rose, a sunflower, a jasmine— it is a water lily! It is finally a water lily; but then it always was, it always had been!

~ *The Sun Is Snowing: Poems, Parables and Pictures*

We're always taught that God wants us to always only say "I can't do this without You God", "Whatever your will is God, that's my will too." But God says He is a father and there is no good father who wants his children to have no will and to think that they can't stand on their own two feet. So maybe what you should be saying is "I can do it" and "I have a strong will, I know what I want." When you think God has left you and wants you to be sitting like a duck; maybe He's actually believing in you, teaching you how to fly.

They say that there are always two kinds of people inside us: one is negative and the other is positive and you have to choose which inner person to listen to. But I have come to recognize that altogether there are three individuals that we carry around with us: one is who we simply are as a creation, as a *being* who is free from influence, who is serene and knowing. The second is the positive and the third is the negative. But I take this even a step further by recognizing that those two other states of existence can actually be seen as separate from you! You should see yourself as the being that you are, as I have explained, and then see the goodness as a friend who is there beside you to believe in you always, to encourage you always. Then the other one is that person who says she's your friend but really isn't your friend and is actually there to cast doubt upon everything about you (everything that you find, know, believe and everything that lights a spark in your heart to lift you up into the sky.) When you see the two as separate entities— you will be able to ground yourself in your own *being,* while knowing that you always have a friend in you. You will always have a friend in you whose eyes are going to light up for yourself! And the fake friend who is always around to cast judgment on you is someone who is actually pitiful. And you don't let pitiful bother you; you let pitiful be pitiful and you just smile at it and you turn to your true friend and you see the spark in her eyes, the joy she has for everything wonderful about you! And that is how one walks through life.

Peace is not a result inside us from everything around us. Peace is neither submissive nor passive. On the contrary, peace is an overwhelming force, which comes from within us, disrespectful of everything around us, a firm coalition of spirit and soul standing against all the unrest that abounds.

I feel like, God expects me to be human. I feel like, God likes me just the way I am: broken and empty and bruised. I feel like, God doesn't look at me and wish that I were something else, because He likes me just this way. I feel like, God doesn't want me to close my eyes and pray for Him to make me holy or for Him to make me pure; because He made me human. I feel like, God already knows I'm human... it is I who needs to learn that.

Ends are not bad things; they just mean that something else is about to begin. And there are many things that don't nd anyway: they just begin again ew way. Ends are not bad and many ends aren't really an ending. Some things are never-ending.

I think humans might be like butterflies. People die every day without many other people knowing about them, seeing their colors, hearing their stories... and when humans are broken, they're like broken butterfly wings: suddenly there are so many beauties that are seen in different ways, so many thoughts and visions and possibilities that form, which couldn't form when the person wasn't broken! So it is not a very sad thing to be broken, after all! It's during the times of being broken that you have all the opportunities to become things unforgettable! Just like the broken butterfly wing that I found which has given me so many thoughts, in so many ways, has shown me so many words and imaginations! But butterflies need to know that it doesn't matter at all if the whole world saw their colors or not! But what matters is that they flew, they glided, they hovered, they saw, they felt and they knew! And they loved the ones whom they flew with! And that is an existence worthwhile!

Our key to greatness lies not in our ability to project ourselves to others as if we are putting ourselves onto a projector and creating an image of ourselves on a projector screen. Rather, our key to greatness lies in who we are which we can give to other people in a way that when they walk away from us, they are able to say in their hearts that they have taken away something with them quite extraordinary.

University can teach you skill and give you opportunity, but it can't teach you sense, nor give you understanding. Sense and understanding are produced within one's soul.

It is only when you accept how different you all are, that you will be able to see how much the same you all are. Don't expect anybody to be the same as you and then you will see that you are in many ways the same as everybody.

A broken soul is not the absence of beauty; but a cracked and torn soul reeks of the sweet incense it contains.

I tell you— the souls of those that are dead— are more alive than some souls of people still living on this earth. There are those who cannot see their own souls, cannot feel their own souls and they breathe and talk and walk around but they are more dead than those who no longer have bodies but who can see themselves, feel themselves and know that they exist! There are more dead walking around than the dead in the graves

I think that fame removes true happiness. Because when you are famous, people know you for who they think you are and when you are happy, it's because people have met you and see you for who you really are. Of course, if you are not a great person, it's

better to be famous. But if you have greatness, it's better to not be famous.

Humanity does not suffer from the disease of wrong beliefs but humanity suffers from the contagious nature of the lack of belief. If you have no magic with you it is not because magic does not exist but it is because you do not believe in it. Even if the sun shines brightly upon your skin every day; if you do not believe in the sunlight— the sunlight for you does not exist.

Some people say they will not believe in anything they can't see. What a catastrophe to not have any faith at all! You live only less than half of a life, if you will only believe in the things that you can see. Life is lived by those who have much faith and believe in many unseen things. If you believe in nothing that you cannot see, think about how much there is that you choose to turn your face away from! You can't see your soul and you cannot prove that it exists, therefore, if you call yourself one who believes in nothing unseen, then you will forever deny your soul its existence, for the existence of the soul dwells in love, trust, anger, passion, faith, belief, strength: the soul is forever nourished by things that are unseen! And so we have too many empty bodies walking around! Bodies with souls inside that are half-dead and dying.

I don't think there are enough words in the world that exist to express exactly just how much I love my son! He's right there in the front of my soul, he can turn me into an eagle, a lioness, a tigress, a swan! A goof or a queen! There's no underestimating just how much I love him! I surround him like the ocean surrounds the ships. I never wanted to change the world until he came along and showed me that he deserves a better world to live in!

You can feel anything. All is free for you to feel. But I guarantee you that if you allow yourself to feel envy and then to swim in it, that envy will destroy you and the people around you. Envy is unlike anger. Envy is neither a right wing nor a left wing, it is not on either end of the balancing beam. Nobody needs it and I can assure you that once you give yourself to it, you will be eaten up! Envy can even eat up nations, casting them up against each other and pull a whole nation down into an internal collapse.

God is colourblind. But we are not God. God does not need to see colour and difference. God is far bigger than all of that. We are human. We are destined to grow and learn from each other and with each other and there is no growing, there is no learning, there is no wonder and no majesty in life if we were like God. We were meant to see colour and difference. To deny these is to lack respect. To blind ourselves to these is to fool one another. To shun these is to deny ourselves growth and knowledge.

Sometimes, you may think you have fallen into an abyss... when in fact you've just descended to the roots... of the tree of life! Somewhere along your climb, you got lost amongst the branches and lost in the darkness of the branches. The only way to find the straight way up would be to return to the roots! And from there amongst the roots, you will be able to look straight up and see the top again! And then begin your ascent!

Maybe we shouldn't begin to stop believing in God when He starts to let go of our hand because at that moment when He begins to let go of your hand— that's the moment He's begun to believe in you! He says: "I believe in you, I know you can." And that's not the time to stop believing in someone— when He is believing in you! A good father knows when to let go and start believing that you can. We may not understand it at first, but afterwards we will look at ourselves and say: "Wow, I'm awesome, I did that all by myself." Then we say "Thanks, dad. If you never let go of me, I would have never learned how to fly."

The problem with thinking that you are the absolute best, is that it leaves no room for you to become any better and while you live life thinking that you're the best; truth is a lot of people around you are already better and becoming even more better.

I'm barely human. I'm more like a creature: to me, everything gives off a scent! Thoughts, moments, feelings, movements, words left unsaid, words barely spoken— they all have a distinct scent, distinct fragrances! Both a smell and a touch! To inhale is to capture, to experience! I can perceive and I can "touch" in so many odd ways! And so I am made up of all these scents, all these feelings! An illumination of nerve endings!

The shame and the downfall of a modern materialistic society is her inability to treasure, care for, admire, adore, cherish, value, revere, respect, uphold, uplift, protect, shield, defend, safeguard, treasure and love her children. I praise all the cultures of this world that naturally harbor and actively manifest these instincts. If a nation or if a population of people fails to recognize the excellent value and distinction of the lives of her children and is defective enough to have lost the capability of expressing and acting upon these instincts then there is nothing that can save that nation or those people. The prosperity of a people is not measured in banks, financial markets, economy, and the death of its humanity is evident not through the loss of life but in the loss of love for its children!

If we come from the water, I conclude that we come from different kinds of it. I will meet a person and in his eyes see an ocean deep and never-ending; then I will meet another person and feel as though I have stepped into a shallow puddle on the street, there is nothing in it. Or maybe some of us come from the water and some of us come from somewhere else, then it's all a matter of finding those who are the same as us.

If you were not cast into the abyss, you would have never groped, reached as far as you could reach, to grasp for anything that you could possibly touch, anything that you could possibly feel brushing against your fingertips! Funny how in the darkness, we come to find the things that we never saw before all the lights departed! It's like someone needed to turn the lights out, to make us find all the things that we never looked for when the lights were on! And it's in that blackness that we wake up to the true light! My friends, curse not the darkness! It has given you many things!

I think that, people are people. That's why the way I treat the lady working in the deli who slices my ham is the same way I treat my friend who drives a Chrysler. That's why the way I treat the guy who packs my groceries is the same way I treat my rich friends. Because people are people. Some are rich and some are poor, and they're all people.

I think people believe empathy to be compassion, that compassion is an inner sense (a sense of the soul.) But empathy is a sense, while compassion isn't a sense. Empathy is an affinity, a communion and a comprehension. They say that empathy is compassion but I think that the two are independent of each other. You see, through empathy you will feel what another is feeling, including all those plans for manipulation and persuasion. You will feel everything, not just the parts that make you take compassion for the person, but also all the red flags! You see, empathy is a sense that works with the other senses such as foresight and intuition. So, we can feel compassion but we have to move with empathy.

One of the best gifts you can give to someone: is a wider perspective. It's also one of the best gifts you can receive. So if you have given someone a wider perspective, don't feel bad about it (about taking their blindfolds off and having to watch them cringe in the newfound sunlight). I know it's hard, but you're doing them a lasting favor. And a wider perspective can be difficult for you yourself to accept, in the beginning (during the time that you squint while the sunlight stings your own eyes); but later you'll find yourself coming back to it, even if you abandoned it as something worthless; you'll look for it one day. Or it will grow on you. Perspective.

The problem with people today, is, they have religions but they have no spirituality. They go to church but they cannot even manage the condition of their own souls. They take pride to state the name of their religions and broadcast these things on Facebook and everywhere, thinking that the nature of their religion represents the nature of their spirit. It's just the same as how they present their cars, houses, and degrees to the world— to stand as a representation of what they are. That's not spirituality; that's still materialism. Yes, perhaps your car, house and degree represents what you've achieved (or what your status in society is); but your religion does not represent what your spirit is like. You cannot go to a certain church or belong to a certain group of people and have that be a replica of your spirit.

Some people center the universe around themselves while making other people nothing but decorations to their existence. "I will do this and then I will do that and then people will think this about me and then people will think that about me, and then I will add that person to my life when the convenient time arrives, and this person over here would make a very convenient addition as well..." They build their own thrones for themselves and add decorations all around their thrones. The problem with that is: it does not bring happiness. A throne must be built for you; it must not be you who builds your own throne. If so, everything that you think you are is only an illusion! And illusions dissolve one day. Poof!

The dance between darkness and light will always remain— the stars and the moon will always need the darkness to be seen, the darkness will just not be worth having without the moon and the stars.

There is no quarrel between science and spirituality. I often hear people of science trying to use it to prove the nonexistence of the spiritual but I simply can't see a chasm in between the two. What is spiritual produces what is scientific, and when science is used to disprove the spiritual, it's always done with the intent to do so: a personal contempt. As a result, scientists today only prove their inferiority to the great founding fathers of the sciences who were practitioners of alchemy. Today's science is washed-out and scrubbed-down, and robbed of everything mystical and spiritual: a knowledge born of contempt and discontent. Or perhaps, there are a few who wish to keep those secrets to themselves and serve everyone else up with a tasteless version of science. And the idiots of today blindly follow their equally blind leaders.

I once knew a man who was heir to the throne of a great kingdom, he lived as a ranger and fought his destiny to sit on a throne but in his blood he was a king. I also knew a man who was the king of a small kingdom, it was very small and his throne very humble but he and his people were all brave and worthy conquerors. And I knew a man who sat on a magnificent throne of a big and majestic kingdom; but he was not a king at all, he was only a cowardly steward. If you are the king of a great kingdom—

you will always be the only king though you live in the bushes. If you are the king of a small kingdom— you can lead your people in worth and honor and together conquer anything. And if you are not a king— though you sit on the king's throne and drape yourself in many fine robes of silk and velvet, you are still not the king and you will never be one.

A clown on a throne is still a clown. A king in rags is still a king.

If you want to change the way that the world appears to be— you must change the way that you see everything in it. And if you want to change the world— you must change the way everyone else sees everything in it. And when everyone else sees everything in the world in a new way— the world will be changed and then mankind will turn their faces to the heavens in search of a brand new vision and then it will be able to see the heavens for what the heavens really are! That being because, in order for a person to change how he sees the world, he must first change the eyes of his soul and it is with those new eyes that man can look at the sun, that man can see the heavens, that man can know God. Then it is with these newfound truths that humanity will continue to live— but living by walking in a new reality.

I continue to marvel at the reluctance of people to look into the mirror and see all the darkness that's within them: all the deceit, the dishonesty, the insincerity, the lack, the need, the want, the lies... they would rather look upon the mural of themselves that they've painted on the wall and stare at that inanimate portrait of beauty, all the while telling themselves that it is the mirror- image of them! This is a falsity, this is unreal! It is only when you turn to the unveiled mirror and bravely face your light and your darkness at once, that you will be able to see the true image of you! How can you pull the thorns from your skin if you are too afraid to open your eyes and look at them? You must open your eyes first, look at the thorns where they are piercing your flesh, and only then can you pull them out!

I don't care what they say; we are only to love those who deserve our love and love them to the degree that they deserve it! You see, we are not God. Only God can love people undeserving without spoiling them. Us, on the other hand, can love someone so undeserving, and actually turn the person into someone so vile who is convinced that they were always entitled to every bit of it! And what about giving? Yes, they all want us to give and expect nothing in return; they all have many scriptures to lie on our tables when it is they who are at the receiving end! But when the tables are turned and we are the ones at the receiving end— suddenly all the scriptures mean something else! And all the times they were on our end and we gave to them— suddenly are all forgotten!

Faith belongs to the human spirit. Faith is faith. Humanity is divided by religion: religion is the divider of humanity. If every human could be removed of their blindfolds and see that faith is in itself faith and that this is something which belongs to each and every human being, then at that time the dividers of religion will suddenly mean nothing and we will all see that we are united by faith in and of itself. There is only one faith and it is called faith. And no man needs to prove to another man that what he believes in exists, because even if it does not exist, his faith is his belief that it is there, that something is there and that in itself is faith. So I do not need to prove to any man that what I believe in exists or not, there is no such contest between man! My faith breathes in the body of my belief: the fact that I believe is the breath of my faith.

No bird in a cage has ever come to know what the mountain winds feel like, by staring at the free flying birds, wishing that they would fall from the sky!

There is a higher form of hierarchy and that is the hierarchy of the spirit. When I stand in front of a person, I stand in front of a soul and I have met magnificent souls in bodies possessing no money, as well as parched and shallow souls in bodies bathed in riches. In the same light, I have met magnificent souls in bodies bathed in wealth, as well as parched and shallow souls in bodies that are impoverished. I am tired of people busying their minds with hierarchy based upon money, because this form of hierarchy is primitive; meanwhile there is an altogether higher form of hierarchy that is of the soul! As you judge man and woman based upon their riches, I laugh at your primitive form of judgment! When I stand in front of a human, I stand in front of a soul.

I've learned, that not all worth is measured by price. I've found so many gems that didn't cost me much!

Many people don't fear a hell after this life and that's because hell is on this earth, in this life. In this life there are many forms of hell that people walk through, sometimes for a day, sometimes for years, sometimes it doesn't end! The kind of hell that doesn't burn your skin; but burns your soul. The kind of hell that people can't see; but the flames lap at your spirit. Heaven is a place on earth, too! It's [illegible] feel freedom, where you're [illegible] No more chains. And you [illegible] your soul laughing.

Our bodies have five senses: touch, smell, taste, sight and hearing. But not to be overlooked are the senses of the soul: intuition, peace, foresight, trust and empathy. The differences between people lie in their use of these senses, most people don't know anything about the inner senses while a few people rely on them just as they rely on their physical senses, and in fact probably even more.

"Because..." he used to cradle his daughter in his arms every morning and often they would exchange soft nuances "...if you can dream it, if you can see it in your visions at night, if you can feel it in your soul, it's yours! And it never really belonged to anyone else, in the first place! It was always yours!" Viera returned her scroll to the drawer and closed it, she kissed the compass around her neck and climbed into her bed under the warm quilts, the candle flame crackled and the memories of her father's arms around her embraced her there in bed and his deep, hoarse voice resounded in her ears, "... and if you chance upon a treasure that is yours and it happens to be in the possession of someone else, it's not very wrong to take what is yours, to take what you dreamed, what you saw in your visions at night, what you felt visit you in your spirit! Sure, it's not lawful, but *aye aye* my little one, listen to me when I tell you that the best things in life are not under the laws of any sort! For which law created love? Which law created courage? The best things, the real things, are the things that are not measured by any man's laws! Fear is the only thing that any law has ever created! And what kind of pirates would we all

be if we were afraid of any of our fears, even a little!"
~ *Dimensions*

I am going to open myself up to all that is superior in the world and beyond and I am going to spend time trying to take delight in things! Not finding ruin in them! If the ruin of you is what you look for, the ruin of you is what you are going to find!

I feel so honored to be able to say: "What I do is for my son," without that being an excuse to do stupid things. No, I will not say that everything I do, I do for God! And no, I will not say that everything I do, I do because I am a sacrificial saint who is in love with people and should be canonized one day! I've heard enough of those lines! It will take the love of a mother to change the world.

When it comes to the education of our young, this privilege should only be given to those whose visions are solely in the uplifting benefit of the child. There is no room for the ego in the education of children! Children should not be looked after, nor educated, by those who have not made a sacrifice within their hearts, laying down their own personal agenda and dreams, for the total ascension of the child. Even if you are to educate the children simply sitting under a tree— if you have the vision and the heart of a sage, those children will grow to be mighty men and women, under your watch! And even if you wine and dine the children, putting them up in a palace, if you do not have the vision and the selfless heart of a sage; all you do is in utter vanity!

Do everything with your whole heart, or not at all. Don't put up with lies or with people who lie to you. Don't risk hurting people just for the fun of it. And lastly, your best foot shouldn't be put forward; it should be with you at all times— right there beside the other one.

The root of all true greatness is humility.

Diamonds are held under tons and tons of pressure, extremely high temperatures of fire and shuffled under shifting of tectonic plates, for a long,

long time! Yet when they come out from there and are put on display for their beauty; does anybody stop to evaluate the diamond based upon all the shit it's been through and say "Remember that disgusting hole it used to be in? I bet it was hell in there!" No, people don't remember where a diamond has come from; they just see the beauty of it now. But it wouldn't have become so beautiful, you know, if not for all of that! So why should we look at other people, or at ourselves and evaluate them/ourselves based upon their/our pasts? Shouldn't we forget that? And only see the beauty that is in front of our eyes? Whatever it was, it made you beautiful! And that is what matters!

Yes, the human race is a small species in an infinite universe filled with many other planets and many other things, but though small; this race is bearer of very great and big things: Destiny, Virtue, Hope, Love... and that's what makes this species different. That's what makes this species very shiny and very visible and very important in a whole, whole, big, big, vast, expanding universe!

I believe that secularism is not the enemy of spirituality. Our spirits are in fact secular and free. But the enemy of your spirit is materialism, which produces legalism. People scramble for the "perfect law" in order fix everything, while failing to see that law only points towards what is material. And so, people find themselves going around in a circle that will never end. The key is to break away from that circle. You have to begin focusing your attention onto what is inside you and what is inside everybody else. This will in turn produce common sense, intuition and understanding. Then comes strength.

It is an extremely unfortunate fact, that there are those who see the morale of respect as something that is beneficial to the other person on the receiving end; rather than something that is beneficial to the one who is capable of giving the respect! It's so unfortunate because that's simply not how it works, the person who is capable of discerning respect and giving it to others, is the person who is better! There are people who believe that the virtue of respect and the ability to discern when to give respect and in which amounts to give it, belongs to the lower class! Oh I beg, I beg to differ! No. And no and no! If I am able to discern the amounts of respect to be given so that I may function as a beaming member of society, this virtue illuminates *me*; this virtue does not illuminate those whom I give the respect to! Respect is known and possessed by the illuminated beings!

There is this certain rawness of soul that puts the polished ones on edge. Some of us just step out and the sunlight illuminates our bones, nerves, veins, and cells! And that's just it, we're just like that! Then the others are tinted, polished, honed and well-contemplated, when they see you walk in and they can see all of your bones, even the tiniest ones— luminous and outlined by the sunlight— it makes them feel shaded-in, it makes them feel hidden, it makes them turn their faces away. The way you bleed yourself all over the lines just makes it too uncomfortable for them, I guess.

The best love in the world is the love of a man. The love of a man who came from your womb, the love of your son! I don't have a daughter, but maybe the love of a daughter is the best too. I am first and foremost me, but right after that I am a mother. The best thing that I can ever be is me. But the best gift that I will ever have is being a mother.

Unfortunately, life is unfair and not all babies are brought into the world with the same amount of anticipation and affection, as others. No matter what anyone says; we are really not all given an equal start at life. And so what must children be made up of, to come into a world like this one? Children must be made up of silk. They must be brought up with serenity in their skin but a bulletproof strength in their souls. This is the new breed of children. Ones that are soft to the touch but are truly unbreakable. And unbreakable in a beautiful way; not in a lost way.

I have learned, that the person I have to ask for forgiveness from the most is: myself. You must love yourself. You have to forgive yourself, everyday, whenever you remember a shortcoming, a flaw; you have to tell yourself "That's just fine." You have to forgive yourself so much until you don't even see those things anymore. Because that's what love is like.

"Tonight I saw Jesus with the eyes on my face. He looks half lion and half man. But not more like a lion and not more like a man; rather the same; I have never seen anything like the face of Jesus before, %100 one thing but %100 another thing: a lion man!"

"Where did you see Him at?"

"On the surface of my blanket as I lay in bed. He was suddenly drawn onto it, like a sketch, and that same moment I knew He was showing His face to me, finally."

"Why do you think He did that?"

"I think He thought it was about time."

We doubt in others, what is in fact in ourselves. The skeletons in your own closet are the things that scare you the most about others. People who come from a background of lying are suspicious of lying in others and so on and so forth. The most trusting of people, are not people who have never been betrayed or who have never felt pain; but the most trusting of people are those who in themselves do not find those things worthy of that blame. We see the world through the eyes of the condition of our own souls.

Go in the direction of where your peace is coming from.

We are all equal in the fact that we are all different. We are all the same in the fact that we will never be the same. We are united by the reality that all colours and all cultures are distinct and individual. We are harmonious in the reality that we are all held to this earth by the same gravity. We don't share blood but we share the air that keeps us alive. I will not blind myself and say that my black brother is not different from me. I will not blind myself and say that my brown sister is not different from me. But my black brother is he as much as I am me. But my brown sister is she as much as I am me.

"Because that happened to me when I was little, this is how I will now treat other people", "Because so and so beat me up and hurt me a long time ago, that gives me the right to treat people the way I treat them, today", "Because life was hard on me, life should be hard on everyone else around me"— does this sound/ look familiar? It's called victim mentality. When people choose to be the direct product of everything that happened to them, the direct product of every single pair of hands that hurt them. And the world, to these people, must bend over backwards in order to accommodate their wounds. Some people don't want to be loved; they just want to make the world pay.

If what you are able to give to others, in this life, is only proportionate to what you received from people in your past—it only means one thing. You are a victim of life's circumstances, a direct and utter equivalent of what has been done to you. Rise above and become more! Be better than what happened to you.

The well from which we draw our love to give to other people, should never be only as deep as the well wherein resides the love we have already received in our lives. The cycle must be broken. The former well must be abandoned and we must create a love in our hearts for others from the bricks and the mortar of our own visions. Our raw materials must come not only from what we received; but our raw materials must come from what we envision to create. From your desires and your visions— your bricks and mortar should materialize. And if your former well is completely empty and dry— so what— you don't owe it to your past, to the people who hurt you, to make that emptiness and that void into your place for drawing water from!

Children must be taught that they are worth being heard, being saved and being loved.

Fairy tales are not real. However, myths are the historical notes of those who were much wiser than ourselves. We therefore have no right to judge legends lest we dare challenge demigods and angels.

I consider myself a stained-glass window. And this is how I live my life. Closing no doors and covering no windows. I am the multi-colored glass with light filtering through me in many different shades, allowing light to shed and fall into many, many hues. My job is not to direct anything, but only to filter into many colors. My answer is destiny and my guide is joy. And there you have me.

I am surely a creature. For what human has two hearts? But I have two hearts—one is always broken; the other is always whole.

B'shert (באַשערט)

(n.) The other part of my soul; soulmate; destiny

You can talk with someone for years, everyday, and still, it won't mean as much as what you can have when you sit in front of someone, not saying a word, yet you feel that person with your heart, you feel like you have known the person for forever... connections are made with the heart, not the tongue.

You only need one man to love you. But him to love you free like a wildfire, crazy like the moon, always like tomorrow, sudden like an inhale and overcoming like the tides. Only one man and all of this.

In this world, it is too common for people to search for someone to lose themselves in. But I am already lost. I will look for someone to find myself in.

They say a good love is one that sits you down, gives you a drink of water and pats you on top of the head. But I say a good love is one that casts you into the wind, sets you ablaze, makes you burn through the skies and ignite the night like a phoenix— the kind that cuts you loose like a wildfire and you can't stop running simply because you keep on burning everything that you touch! I say that's a good love— one that burns and flies, and you run with it!

The only love for me is a love that's loved with everything. With every fire. With every flame. With every breath. With every drop of blood. With every thought. With every blink of the eye. With every bit of time. And if a love is not loved with all of this and more— it is somebody else's; it is not my own.

She didn't belong anywhere and she never really belonged to anyone. And everyone else belonged somewhere and to someone. People thought she was too wonderful. But she only wanted to belong to someone. People always thought she was too wonderful to belong to them or that something too wonderful would hurt too much to lose. And that's why she liked him— because he just thought she was crazy.

If I am to be fallen into love, I will. And if as a result I will appear to be stupid, disillusioned, and of poor judgment, I will. And I would be damned if I cared what other people think. For I would rather be thought of as all of these things, than not love. If in loving, I become the naked woman on the horse, I will ride that horse with my head held high. This is my spirit. I am unbreakable.

You will manage to keep a woman in love with you only for as long as you can keep her in love with the person she becomes when she is with you.

When you look for a man, what you want to look for is a man with a heart full of humility and a mind full of victory.

And suddenly I saw him with me, everywhere! In all of the memories I long to create, in all of the places that I long to be— every place where there was a piece of my heart— I suddenly saw him there, beside me! In London and at the Trevi Fountain in Rome, New York City at midnight and Paris at dawn! Laughing with me, holding my hand... inseparable.

I have learned that you can go anywhere you want to go and do anything you want to do and buy all the things that you want to buy and meet all the people that you want to meet and learn all the things that you desire to learn and if you do all these things but are not madly in love— you have still not begun to live.

Before, I wanted to say: "I found love!" But now, I want to say: "I found a person. And he belongs to me and I belong to him."

I cannot have a man who is afraid of everything, I don't have the time to soothe insecurities and fears, I cannot have a man who is standing on a stone by a creek, watching for the fish to swim by and every time he sees a fish he says: "Oh look, this fish scares me, I wonder what this fish means, this fish might mean this, or this fish might mean that" for God's sake, they are just fish and they don't mean anything! Such a sad thing, so many fine, strong men standing on top of little stones, pointing at fish all the time! Such a waste! Such a waste of time! I can only have a man who will leap into the water, not minding the damn fish and whatever other little things that scare him. I need to have someone who is braver than me! If I am a pirate, he has to be the pirate Captain, if I am a pirate Captain he has to be the flying dragon.

I don't understand dating... and the other things that people do... all I know is that you ought to find the one you recognize. The one who gives you four arms, four legs, four eyes and has the other half of your heart. There's only one of those, so what are all the other things for? Like dating?

"How could you love us being together?" he asked me.

"We are nothing alike and we are not meant for each other and we drive each other crazy, you love that? How can you love that?"

So I told him "I know that we're not meant for each other, that we drive each other crazy and that we are so different. But that's us. That's what we have— a wild nonsense. We are not good together, but together we are bad for each other. I love us together this way just like this. Because even if it's no good, it's what we have! It's us."

It should be a privilege to be able to say, "I love you" to someone. It shouldn't be something people say just because they feel like it. It is a privilege that is earned. They say you have to earn the right to be loved; no, love is unconditional and if you love someone, they don't have to earn it. But. The right to tell someone that you love them? That has to be earned. You have to earn the right to be believed.

Sometimes the things that are felt the most are expressed between two souls over the distance and over time... where no words abide. And others may speak freely, live with one another freely, express themselves freely— just like everyone else, but then there is you... you have no words for proof of reassurance, no tokens of professed love, but you have something. Something worth keeping.

~ *Saint Paul Trois Châteaux: 1948*

If people are going to be allowed to say "we love you" and "I love you", they'd better have the backbone to prove it. Love isn't just a word.

If you find a man who trusts you, who isn't afraid, who sees you for who you are and if it feels like he knows you for who it is that you simply are and thinks all of that is beautiful—know that you have found a rare thing.

Love is like a good cake: you never know when it's coming but you'd better eat it when it does!

Maybe we shouldn't be looking for love. Maybe we should be looking for a person. Because maybe you can find love in a person, but not have that person. So if you look for love, what you will find is love. But if you want to belong to someone and you want someone to belong to you— you should look for a person.

The only thing that will ever make me fall in love is: if I fall in love.

The mark of a real man is a man who can allow himself to fall deeply in love with a woman. But the reason why a man is often heartbroken is because a woman can be overcome by the reality that she has made a man out of a boy, because it's just such an overwhelming process, a beautiful and powerful evolution. Therefore, a man needs to fall in love with a woman who knows that men don't happen every day, and when a man does happen, that's a gift! A gift not always given and one that shouldn't be thrown away so easily.

They were from two different worlds. Two entirely different people. But upon their coming together, they created— they found— their own path and together they had their own world and in their own world, they were the same. Everyone else outside of it— everyone else was over there. Away. And they together— they together were here. They were right here. They were the same.

I have met so many heartbroken men. It's a catastrophe. Women are easily overcome by the process that happens when a boy falls in love and becomes a man. Men's hearts are so often broken. Still, you have to leave your broken heart in a place where— when the woman who knows how to see what a gift is, sees it— your broken heart can be picked up again. I think that it takes a very strong woman (inner strength) to be able to handle a man falling in love with her, without morphing into a monster (the process is a very potent process, it can poison a woman, really). A woman thinks she wants a man to fall in love with her for all the perks that come with it; but when a true love really does happen, when a real man shows his manhood; it's often too powerful a thing to endure without being poisoned. Hence: all the heartbroken men. But, I do believe that there are strong women in the world today. A few. But there are. You could say that the mark of a real woman is a woman who can handle a man falling in love with her. A woman who can recognize that and keep it with her.

The real thing that keeps men and women apart is fear. Women blame men and men blame women, but the culprit is fear, women are afraid of one thing, men are afraid of a different thing. The fears of women have to do with losing while the fears of men have to do with not being good enough for something. One is loss while the other is insecurity. Men are innately more insecure than women and women are innately more needful of companionship than men. It's good for both men and women to be able to recognize and identify these fears not only within themselves, but also within each other, and then men and women will see that they really do need to help one another. It's not a game, it's not a competition, the two sexes need one another.

You deserve to be with somebody who knows you're the one from that very first moment he lays eyes on you. Do I believe in love at first sight? E course! Love cannot be tamec bridled by things like time, circumstance and logic!

You can see the whole entire world in the eyes of a person who knows how to simply stand there and take all of it into him but then you can look into the eyes of someone else and the whole entire world goes away and all that's left is you.

~ *Saint Paul Trois Châteaux: 1948*

I think that you can meet someone one day, who possesses the eyes you never had but always needed, the vision to see backwards and forwards and all around, the other wing that you need to complete your flight. And I think it can just happen, suddenly, without explanation! And then I think, it would be good to keep that person because you'll always have those eyes and always have two wings.

Thus is the nature of love: that you must use it! A love unused is not love! If it is something that sits on the shelf that you don't know what to do with, then it is not true to the nature of love! Use love!

The coward says in his heart "There is no love." Because, standing in the shadows of the big, grand and powerful existence of love, his small spirit is left feeling even smaller and less significant. And so he chooses to deny the existence of love altogether. Because he is too small to have it.

The journey to a thousand stars is not too far a journey in the quest to have true love abiding in a pure heart.

It was him, it was always him, and they only needed to stand there with their feet buried into the muddy moss and look at each other to feel each other. Time stopped, movement disappeared and it was both the beginning of everything and the end of everything else. They had each other and there was no name, no title to it other than they just had each other. There was no necessity to be practical. What they had and what they were, was of their own and in their own and I think nothing in the world could have made Lucy happier than to have what they had, to be what they were.

~ *Saint Paul Trois Châteaux: 1948*

When I laugh, I desire to laugh in all the intensity of pure joy. When I cry, I want to cry in all the sincerity of the heart. When I scream— be it at the top of my lungs— or else not scream at all. And when I love, I wish to love in all the manners of the Heavens and the earth and everything else in between.

Many people do not fall in love; they fall in love with the idea of themselves being in love. They never see the other person. I don't ask for much— I only ask to be seen.

"Where are you?" he asked. "I'm right here," she said. "I know, but it feels like one percent of you is somewhere else, where is that one percent?" he said. "I don't know... I think I'm always like that..." she answered. "I like that." "You do?" "Yes, because that way, I have to always look for the one percent to find it."

Sometimes you want to stay with someone not only because it's magic and it's promising and it feels like home; but sometimes you find someone and you want to stay with him (or her) because you're the same kind of animal.

You can run away from yourself so often and so much, just because the broken pieces of you cut your feet too deeply if you stay around for too long. But then what if someone were to come along and pick up those pieces for you? Then you wouldn't have to run away from yourself anymore. You could stop running. If someone sees you as something worth staying with— maybe you'll stay with yourself, too.

There's that day when you realize that everything that happened before that one person found you, probably happened to prepare you and to prepare everything for that person's arrival. It's not that everything suddenly "makes sense" but it's more that you understand why this didn't work and that didn't work and why you fell into this ditch and you broke a certain bone somewhere. It's so they'd find you. Or so that you'd find them. So you'd find each other.

I have always been a lone wolf and in the real sense of the word (people say it all the time but it's usually not true.) I feel like I watch people and I wonder why they do things. Especially when it comes to love and relationships, most of the time I am thinking, "Why are they together when they are not meant to be together?" but then I realize that they don't know that they're not meant to be together! And I don't see any importance in all the other reasons why people usually want to be together—because it looks good, because it's convenient, because it's a fun game to play... the only reason to be with someone is if you are meant for someone. You're a wolf and they're a wolf too and you look at each other and you say, "You're my family, you're my home." Well, that's how I think.

When you trust and you lose— it is because you were wrong to trust and what you believed was merely a phantom. But when you doubt and you lose— it is because in your wanting so much not to be wrong, you lost something that was entirely beautiful for you. More is lost, in the end, by those who doubt. I would rather lose the phantom.

The most important things in a romantic relationship are compromise, honesty, openness, humility and trust. If you don't have these with someone, you don't have anything.

So, I believe that what you are looking for, really looking for, is that one person who is capable of recognizing you no matter what. You know, that one person who is going to be able to see past what everybody else sees and even past what you yourself see or want to show, then be able to look at you and really recognize you and say: "That's not you! This is you right over here! You just forgot yourself, but I see you! I will help you remember yourself, because I remember you!" And that's what everyone wants. No, actually, I don't know if that's what everyone wants; but I know that's what I want! Because I can put up so many damn walls and faces just to see who really knows me, who really recognizes me, who really remembers me, even more than I recognize and remember myself! Because if I don't get that, then I don't get anything, because I don't want anything less than that.

There's that kind of love you don't want to say anything about. You want to be quiet about it, be hush about it, and not say a word about it. And why? Well only because you don't want to bother it in any way, because you just might do something a little wrong to it. It's like the perfect snowflake that lands on your eyelash— and then you just stop moving.

Backpfeifengesicht

(n.) lit. “a face that needs a fist in it”

The difference between my darkness and your darkness is that I can look at my own badness in the face and accept its existence while you are busy covering your mirror with a white linen sheet. The difference between my sins and your sins is that when I sin I know I'm sinning while you have actually fallen prey to your own fabricated illusions. I am a siren, a mermaid: I know that I am beautiful while basking on the ocean's waves and I know that I can eat flesh and bones at the bottom of the sea. You are a white witch, a wizard: your spells are manipulations and your cauldron from hell yet you wrap yourself in white and wear a silver wig.

When I see you, I think: "I wonder which face she sees when she looks into the mirror."

Too many people are endowed with a feeling of entitlement, but born without God-given empathy.

Hypocrisy annoys me. People need to look into mirrors. Let me hold a mirror in front of your face.

There are people who are generic. They make generic responses and they expect generic answers. They live inside a box and they think people who don't fit into their box are weird. But I'll tell you what; generic people are the weird people. They are like genetically manipulated plants growing inside a laboratory, like indistinguishable faces, like droids. Like ignorance.

Be careful not to mistake insecurity and inadequacy for humility! Humility has nothing to do with the insecure and inadequate! Just like arrogance has nothing to do with greatness!

When I was little and running on the racetrack at school, I always stopped and waited for all the other kids so we could run together even though I knew (and everybody else knew) that I could run much faster than all of them! And I pretended to read slowly so I could "wait" for everyone else who couldn't read as fast as I could! When my friends were short I pretended that I was short too and if my friend was sad I pretended to be unhappy. I could go on and on about all the ways I have limited myself, my whole life, by "waiting" for people. And the only thing that I've ever received in return is people thinking that they are faster than me, people thinking that they can make me feel bad about myself just because I let them and people thinking that I have to do whatever they say I should do. My mother used to teach me "Cinderella is a perfect example to be" but I have learned that Cinderella can go fuck herself because I'm not waiting for anybody, anymore! I'm going to run as fast as I can, fly as high as I can, I am going to soar! And if you want you can come with me! But I'm not waiting for you anymore.

I remember a relative of mine who used to pick on me all the time, constantly ridiculing my every move and making me feel inferior. One day she had a pimple on her face and was devastated. I told her "Why would you let a little thing like that bother you in such a way? It's just a pimple!" And she cried and said "You can say that, because you're perfect and even if you have ten pimples on your face, it wouldn't even matter!" And I never forgot how I felt in that moment— that moment taught me some important things! First, I realized that the whole time she was picking on me, she actually was feeling that I was perfect! And secondly, I realized that when people think you're perfect, they try to make you feel bad about yourself! I was so taken aback in those few minutes, I couldn't even say anything! I just looked at her while all my realizations flooded my mind and I decided that just because you think someone is perfect, doesn't give you the ticket to make them feel bad about themselves.

Don't let a thief into your house three times. The first time was enough. The second time was a chance. The third time means you're stupid.

I am an extremely sincere individual. I am sincere, to a fault. One of the many things that I have come to realize, to learn, is that sincerity must be reserved and given only to those who deserve it. And one must save one's emotions, channeling them only to the people who are worthy of it. One must not throw one's pearls to the pigs.

There are those whose primary ability is to spin wheels of manipulation. It is their second skin and without these spinning wheels, they simply do not know how to function. They are like toys on wheels of manipulation and control. If you remove one of the wheels, they'll never be able to feel secure, be whole.

If you swim effortlessly in the deep oceans, ride the waves to and from the shore, if you can breathe under water and dine on the deep treasures of the seas, mark my words— those who dwell on the rocks carrying nets will try to reel you into their catch. The last thing they want is for you to thrive in your habitat because they stand in their atmosphere where they beg and gasp for some air.

If you walk on sunlight, bathe in moonlight, breathe in a golden air and exhale a Midas' touch, mark my words— those who exist in the shadows will try to pull you into the darkness with them. The last thing that they want is for you to see the wonder of your life because they can't see theirs.

It's not unfortunate that people aren't genuine; what's unfortunate is that insincere people try to act sincere and in doing so, mislead and deceive the other. I would rather meet a person who is not amiable and who does not feel any burden to act amiable towards me, than to have the misfortune of knowing people who feel like they need to be gracious and compassionate so they will appear to be good people, whilst possessing none of those qualities within themselves! It's the latter that causes the pain in life. And that's another reason why I don't believe in religion: I have observed that religion tells people that it is highly prized a quality to act kind and compassionate and so on and so forth, but some people just do not have these innate qualities within them! We get deceived and I'd rather not be deceived! I'd rather be able to see a person for who he/she is and not judge a brute for being a brute, but avoid the brute who carries the burden of acting like a wonderful one!

If you are stealing people's thunder just by being around and standing there, you really can't expect people to like you. People want their own thunder to be heard loud and wide; not yours! Swans should never despair over ducks not liking them.

If Cinderella were given a single shining epiphany (instead of a fairy godmother), she would have realized: "This is my father's house. This is my father's estate. I am the rightful heiress to everything here!" then she would have said: "Get off of my property, take nothing with you and never show your faces to me again! You ugly, bitter, insecure, envious witches!" And I'm sure she would have been happier, sooner!

Silk is a fine, delicate, soft, illuminating, beautiful substance. But you can never rip it! If a man takes this tender silk and attempts to tear it and cannot tear it, is he in his right mind to say, "This silk is fake! I thought it was soft, I thought it was delicate, but look, I cannot even tear it!" Surely, this man is not in his right mind! The silk is not fake! This silk is 100% real. It's the man who is stupid!

Some people walk through a hallway with covered mirrors. The hallway is lined with mirrors but there are blankets covering each of them. They go through life believing in an image of themselves that isn't real, and an image of themselves standing in the world and relative to the world, that isn't real. If you happen to be in that hallway and pull the blankets off the mirrors, they're going to think that you're hurting them; but they're actually just seeing their reflection for the first time. Sometimes the most horrendous things a person can see are all the hidden things inside them, the things they've covered, the things they choose not look at! And you're not hurting them; you're setting them free.

I was just thinking... how it is not and it will never be okay to cause pain in someone's life just because of the fact that you are envious of them! Is someone taller than you? Richer than you? More beautiful? That doesn't make it okay to hurt those people, for all you know, they bear deep wounds and carry heavy burdens and their heartache is far greater than anything you could ever bear! People try to hurt people that they're envious of, without knowing that they are adding to what is already painful. And because someone has more than you or has what it is that you want, doesn't mean that they owe you anything! It's not their fault! Be careful, you may just be wounding an angel soul and a wound inflicted upon an angel soul will always, always come back to haunt *you.*

Open your mind to the world and the many different ways that can be found in it, before making hasty judgments of others. After all, the very same thing that you judge from where you are—may very well be something totally different in meaning on the other side of the world. The problem with making hasty judgments is that it will emphasize your ignorance at the end of the day.

Stop right there, don't judge. Ask first. Open your mouth or type in that text message. Ask questions.

There are just those faces that really need a good slapping. They're usually smiling at you, quietly manipulating you from behind the bashful grins. See those naïve eyes? They hide a mind that wants to steal everything away from you and leave you in a pile of dead dogs!

Philocaly

(n.) The love of beauty.

I can't decide whether I'm a good girl wrapped up in a bad girl; or if I'm a bad girl wrapped up in a good girl. And that's how I know I'm a woman!

The strength of a woman is not measured by the impact that all her hardships in life have had on her; but the strength of a woman is measured by the extent of her refusal to allow those hardships to dictate her and who she becomes.

It's not very easy to grow up into a woman. We are always taught, almost bombarded, with ideals of what we should be at every age in our lives: "This is what you should wear at age twenty", "That is what you must act like at age twenty-five", "This is what you should be doing when you are seventeen." But amidst all the many voices that bark all these orders and set all of these ideals for girls today, there lacks the voice of assurance. There is no comfort and assurance. I want to be able to say, that there are four things admirable for a woman to be, at any age! Whether you are four or forty-four or nineteen! It's

always wonderful to be elegant, it's always fashionable to have grace, it's always glamorous to be brave and it's always
important to own a delectable perfume! Yes, wearing a beautiful fragrance is in style at any age!

Elegance is a glowing inner peace. Grace is an ability to give as well as to receive and be thankful. Mystery is a hidden laugh always ready to surface! Glamour only radiates if there is a sublime courage and bravery within: glamour is like the moon— it only shines because the sun is there.

I used to feel so insecure about myself because I always just stood out from everyone, all the time. I never looked like anyone else around me, not even anyone in my family! In photographs I would just look like this different kind of creature embossed onto the background— my eyes were always burning and my skin was always glowing and in my opinion, my mouth was too big and I looked like a wild thing! It's taken me decades to realize that I should have never bent over or conformed to anything or anyone around me. I could have been who I was and that would have been the most beautiful thing! I should have always allowed myself to be my own kind of beautiful.

Beauty and grace walk hand-in-hand. Show me grace and I will show you true beauty. Show me true beauty and I will show you grace. It is impossible for the one to exist in the absence of the other.

Ideally, no woman in the world should be forced into strength. Unfortunately, life's circumstances take the gentlest of us and force us into taking up shield and sword. Women are forced into becoming strong. The beautiful and wondrous this is how the slightest amount of true appreciation, affection, love, can be like silk against the skin—someone who sees and knows your worth and tries to show that to you—can swathe you in silk, make you feel beautiful, make you feel happy.

It's definitely difficult being a woman and growing up a girl. When you're graceful, people say you lack personality; when you're serene, people say you're boring; when you're confident, people say you're arrogant; when you're feminine, people say you're too girly; and when you climb trees, people say you're too much of a tomboy! As a woman, you really need to develop a very strong sense of self and the earlier you can do that, the better! You have to be all the things that you are, without allowing other people's ignorance change you! I realized that they don't know what grace is, they can't identify serenity, they have inferiority complexes, they are incapable of being feminine, and they don't know how to climb trees!

The only problem with her is that she is too perfect. She is bad in a way that entices and good in a way that comforts. She is mischief; but then she is the warmth of home. The dreams of the wild and dangerous; but the memories of childhood and gladness. She is perfection. And when given something perfect, it is the nature of man to dedicate his mind to finding something wrong with it and then when he is able to find something wrong with it, he rejoices in his find and sees only the flaw, becoming blind to everything else! And this is why man is never given anything that is perfect, because when given the imperfect and the ugly, man will dedicate his mind to finding what is good with the imperfect and upon finding one thing good with the extremely flawed, he will only see the one thing good and no longer see everything that is ugly. And so... man complains to God for having less than what he wants... but this is the only thing that man can handle. Man cannot handle what is perfect. It is the nature of the mortal to rejoice over the one thing that he can proudly say that he found on his own with no help from another, whether it be a shadow in a perfect diamond, or a faint beautiful reflection in an extremely dull mirror.

Do not yearn to be popular; be exquisite. Do not desire to be famous; be loved. Do not take pride in being expected; be palpable, unmistakable.

There are diamonds in the rough that will always be shunned by the stones lying around them.

Society tells men that the way to a woman's heart is by making her feel like she can't have him and has to chase him. This is stupidity and is only applicable to stupid women. If I feel like I will have to chase a man because I can't have him— Goodbye coward, hello better man! 'Tis a hero's heart I seek. Not a fish swimming around that I have to catch. What will I do with a fish?

I am not a little bit of many things; but I am the sufficient representation of many things. I am not an incompletion of all these races; but I am a masterpiece of the prolific. I am an entirety, I am not a lack of anything; rather I am a whole of many things. God did not see it needful to make me generic. He thinks I am better than that.

Peace is the number one beautiful ornament you can wear, I really believe that. They say you should always wear a smile, but I don't believe that you should "always" wear a smile, seriously, you're going to look stupid! But peace—you should always carry peace within you because it is the most beautifying thing you could ever have or do. Peace makes your heart beautiful and it makes you look beautiful, too. You want to have perfect physical posture when you stand, sit and walk, and peace is the perfect posture of the soul, really. Try perfect posture outside as well as inside. Peace creates grace and grace gives peace.

I believe in strong women. I believe in the woman who is able to stand up for herself. I believe in the woman who doesn't need to hide behind her husband's back. I believe that if you have problems, as a woman you deal with them, you don't play victim, you don't make yourself look pitiful, you don't point fingers. You stand and you deal. You face the world with a head held high and you carry the universe in your heart.

Grace is what picks me up and lifts my wings high above and I fly! Grace always conquers! Be graceful in everything: in anger, in sadness, in joy, in kindness, in unkindness— retain grace with you!

I would rather carry around a plastic bag with five thousand Euros inside, than carry around a Louis Vuitton/Gucci/Prada bag with only one hundred Euros inside of it!

Women waste so much time wearing no perfume. As for me, in every step that I have taken in life, I have been accompanied by an exquisite perfume!

I'm half good and I'm half bad. My mama is a very good girl and my daddy is a very bad boy. And I guess that leaves me somewhere sort of... here.

I come across too much material on "how to make a man want you", "how to make a man commit", "how to make a man finally pop the question", "how to make a man take you seriously", "how to get into a man's emotions." And I laugh. My dear fellow women, enough! Do not busy yourselves with such things! Instead, fall in love with yourself!

You are never fully dressed without perfume!

Inside every woman, is a crazy girl. And we all know what I'm talking about. That part of you that is entangled with insecurities, fears and absolute insanity! The art of femininity lies in the molding, pounding and defeating of that crazy girl on a daily basis! Look at any woman, and you're looking at a woman fighting a daily battle, wielding her weapons in war, every day! I have said it before and I'll say it again: it is never easy being a woman! And if we could only pound that crazy, insecure girl out of ourselves— it would make such the difference!

Young girls today are very mistaken to be thinking that their sense of self-worth and their acknowledgment of their beauty depends on whether a man will give that to them or not. Such naïveté! And so what will happen when the man changes his mind about her? Tells her she's not beautiful enough? That she's not good enough? Cheats on her? Leaves her? Then what happens? She will lose all her self-worth, she will think she is not good enough, she is not beautiful enough, because all of those feelings depended on the man in the first place! And along with the loss of the man, it will all be lost as well! Mothers, teach your daughters better. It pains me to see such naive innocence right under my nose! Such naïveté does no good for any girl. It is better for a girl to be worldly-wise and have street smarts! That's what a girl needs to have in life! Not wide-eyed delusional innocence! The sense of self-worth and acknowledgment of being beautiful must not come from a man; it must come from inside the woman herself because men will come and men will go and their coming and going must not take an effect on the woman's sense of worth and beauty.

Today I wondered why my eyelashes aren't thick enough and why my feet aren't small enough. Then it hit me. Why do we take these insignificant things like millimeters on lashes and shoeboxes and then try to fit ourselves into those stupid molds? Why do I take the beauty that is me and measure it up to a shoe size? A length of hair on my eyelids? Am I not the more wonderful creation, far greater in worth than those stupid things? Why do we take ourselves and desecrate ourselves daily? Pushing ourselves into cubicles because we think we are supposed to fit into them? Are we ice cubes? And suddenly I just don't understand the inadequacies anymore! Because they're not even inadequacies at all! I will laugh and be beautiful.

She laughs an honest laugh... one that puts the fakes on edge and makes them dream of being better.

Pink is a beautiful color because it is one of the colors that the sun makes at twilight and in the dawns.

It's easy to make me laugh! You can make me laugh, anyone can make me laugh, but that certainly does not mean you can make me do anything.

I can't over-emphasize how important an exquisite perfume is, to be wrapped and cradled in an enchanting scent upon your skin is a magic all on its own! The notes in that precious liquid will remind you that you love yourself and will tell other people that they ought to love you because you know that you're worth it.

The love affair created by a good perfume between you and other people, you and nature, you and yourself, you and your memories and anticipations and hopes and dreams: it is all too beautiful a thing!

Perfection: a collection of a variety of pieces that, when viewed and felt individually, are difficult and confusing; but when brought together as one, create a perfect picture. Symphony, harmony, serenity.

The fragrance of white tea is the feeling of existing in the mists that float over waters; the scent of peony is the scent of the absence of negativity: a lack of confusion, doubt and darkness; to smell a rose is to teach your soul to skip; a nut and a wood together is a walk over fallen Autumn leaves; the touch of jasmine is a night's dream under the nomad's moon.

At times, I really am just a girl who dreams of holding hands with a handsome man, traveling with a handsome man, eating gelato with a handsome man, laughing with and kissing— a handsome man! Oh so many of my dreams are filled with a handsome man! And nice shoes. Oh I couldn't be with a handsome man and be wearing ugly shoes!

There is no need to always require a smile! Happiness is more of a look in the eyes, than a smile on the face!

Some of us are crèmes brûlées, unfortunately in the presence of those who would rather have corn dogs. We can try to degenerate into corn dogs to make them happy, or we can just accept the fact that we were made for Paris!

When you are a real queen, there is absolutely no reason to try and make people believe that you are one. Because you just are. Life is lived with grace, courage and serenity. If you must dedicate any amount of time and mental ability to making anyone believe that you are one— you're not!

I do wonder why people hate their grey hair so much! I think grey hair is a gift from the moon! When the moon laughs, her eyes produce tears of joy that fall to the earth and onto the tops of people's heads!

Coco Chanel used to talk about wearing more than one string of pearls. Why wear one if you can wear two, or something to that effect. I think that one string of pearls is just fine. But that's because my pearls are black; hers were white.

If the world were to come to an end tomorrow, I would still buy that tube of Chanel lipstick today.

Class is grace, grace is class.

We all have our indulgences. Some women indulge in expensive shoes, lots of my friends indulge in expensive bags, others are really into jewellery pieces; but I— I have my lipstick! Of course women usually have a little of all these things, but we tend to splurge in one area: some of us are "bag girls" while others are "shoe girls"; I'm a makeup girl! My friends sit their designer handbags on their laps when they're stressed; I just pull out my powder and powder away! I have all kinds of powders: some are lilac, some are peach, some are a mixture of lilac and peach and green and pink (really)! And there's nothing more comforting than pulling out the perfect shade of pink lipstick in the middle of the sidewalk and applying it right there in that moment you need it the most! For me, it is my way of reminding time and space that whenever I want to— I can make it stop! Because none of that will matter, not even a little, when I pull my lipstick out! The world may melt over under lava for all I care! I will wear my expensive lipstick!

What we become shouldn't be dictated by the mud and the dung and the dust and the fire and the ice and the dirt and the spit that hit us in the face, but what we become must be a choice made every day in the heart and they who threw all of that at us to try and defile us— they will look up at us and see us no less beautiful. And even more beautiful.

She has a serene, glowing disposition. She looks at you and the rest of the world through the eyes of a lynx and is always mysterious, possibly because she always harbours those hidden laughs just beneath her lips. She's always ready to laugh.

I am not interested in having the world revolve around me; that's too boring of an idea. I would rather revolve around the world and try to leave my fingerprints everywhere! My fingerprints mingled in with all the other fingerprints and all the laughter and all the beautiful things like gratitude, grace, faithfulness and flowers.

There are blue diamonds born to the world and given to those who only want glass crystals. There are blue roses born to the world yet given to those who only want daisies. Blue diamond; don't cry because they want glass crystals. Blue rose, don't bleed because they see only the daisies. You were formed in the bedroom of the gods, you were conceived in the garden of the eternal!

Beauty without grace is like a fish far displaced from the water and looking at this kind of beauty is like watching that fish die right there on the cement in front of you.

Sometimes, I miss so much the person that I was before the world tore me up in so many places. If only "they" could have just let me stay that way.

I will laugh and be beautiful. And if anyone thinks I'm a damned fool, they're welcome to come and discover even more damned things about me.

People think that the word "class" involves the color black, wearing Chanel No. 5 and carrying around a Louis Vuitton. The word "class" and "classy", to me, mean what happens when you are able to be thankful, able to give and be a true friend to anybody regardless of their background and where they come from. That's class. It's a beautiful wave that washes away faults and paints things in a graceful light. You can't always do this, though. Sometimes you just need to slap someone. Still, you can slap someone with a lot of poise and that makes all the difference.

As women, we are always taught never to let a man know of our affections towards him, lest he laugh, run away, or think that we are psycho. But what if that's not true? Have you ever stopped to think that? What if it's like there's a beautiful little bird in our hearts and we're too afraid to let anyone see it in there? What's wrong with letting anyone know that there's a bird in your chest? Maybe there are lots of wrong ones; but maybe there's one that is just for you—the one who won't laugh or run away when he sees that little bird. After all, it's just a pretty bird!

Because she looks to the sky so often, people think that her life is sweet, that her eyes are dotted with dreamy stars. But quite the opposite is true and I wish

— she looks up so much ound her it's hard to see ting her heart. She once a window sign that said: "We're all in the gutter; but some of us are looking at the stars." From that movie onwards, she decided to look up! Doesn't mean her life is sweet, doesn't mean her eyes are dotted with dreamy stars.

God is funny. He had a funny day when he made me. A funny, thoughtful, crazy day. He gave me a physique by which I would be so easily and so quickly judged, then gave me a mind by which I would so deeply magnetize, He put within me a heart with small, fast wings that I can hardly, barely handle, and then gave me a voice that hides behind everything in whispers. Oh, and also put a pen in my hand, which writes me into madness! How can anyone possibly understand me? But I don't think God cared about that thought, when He made me! How ridiculously unfair!

The one who is born of the earth, dreams of the sky. The one who is born of the sky, dreams of the earth.

I believe in roses. Oh God, yes! I do believe in roses! And I believe in lots and lots and lots of them, too!

I believe in roses. And I believe in putting roses into a vase and sitting the vase on the table. I believe in getting lost and being found, I believe in going barefoot, and in laughter! My religion is to laugh at myself, whenever I can! I believe in the sunlight and in grey skies with big, beautiful clouds!

My religion consists of laughing at myself. My motto is this: As long as there is a me, there is a reason to laugh out loud!

I think that the trademark of the Devil in this world is the awful rift between women. Women backbiting other women, women envying other women and so on and so forth. And then there is the telltale sign of God in this world, which is the intoxicating potion of joy that is concocted when a woman reaches out to another woman, when women will take an extra step, go an extra mile, or just go out of their way an inch for their fellow woman, regardless of the varying degrees of things we hold important such as beauty, intelligence, status and so on and so forth. Beautiful acts of God are seen in the kindness of women towards other women.

Ichariba Chode
行逢りば兄弟

(phr.) "Though we meet but once, if only by chance, we are like brothers and sisters for life."

There are still some wonderful people left in this world! They are diamonds in the rough, but they're around! You'll find them when you fall down— they're the ones who pick you up, who don't judge, and you had to fall down to see them! When you get up again, remember who your true friends are!

There are two kinds of friendship: the beneficial friendship and the erroneous friendship. The erroneous friendship balances on the principle of "the closer we are, the more okay it is for me to say anything I want to you and for me to treat you any way that I want to, and for me to disrespect you and take advantage of you" while a true friendship is rooted in this principle: "the closer we are, the more respect I have for you, the better I will treat you, the higher I will regard you, the more good things I will wish for you." You will know someone is a true friend by basis of observing his or her actions towards you, as the friendship grows deeper. A true friend will continue to hold you in higher and higher regard while the error of a friend will see your goodwill and newfound fondness as basis to do and say whatever he/she wants, that is disrespectful and non-beneficial to you.

I really like the thing called friendship. And I think the most fulfilling kind of friendship is the one that you stumble quite randomly upon. Unexpected and unknown. You can learn a lot about yourself from these kinds of friendships, and some last a long time while others last only for the duration of time that you have together! But then I wonder, is the length of a friendship measured by the time you are given to spend within each other's company? Or is it measured by how long into the future you can look back at the photos you took, look back and replay the adventures and the laughter in your mind, while still feeling like it was one of the "bestest" times of your life? Because if it's the latter, I have a thousand friends!

Friendship is so important. The goal of a good friendship should be for life! To keep it for life! If you find a friendship and it gives you a joy inside, a peace, and a freedom— keep that friendship for life. Through it all, you stay together. So many friendships are toxic; but the good ones are really good! I always tell my son this, I always say: a friend is for life!

I cannot hate gay men, I cannot hate homosexuality. At the lowest points in my life, when all else abandoned me, my gay men friends were my sisters, aunts, mothers who lifted me up on their shoulders and reminded me that there is light at the end of the tunnel. If I were to hate gay men, or to condemn them just because they're gay, I would be a hypocrite. I simply cannot turn my back on arms that held me in my darkest hours.

Perhaps there really is a good that exists, for a century of darkness to be eschewed by a single flame, for a decade of evil done to the heart to be undone by simple and unplanned acts of kindness! There must be a goodness, after all! But we don't find it when we're looking for it; not in church, not in a cathedral, not even in our own homes! We find it when we've fallen down so hard, are downtrodden so low and there is one true friend who picks us up or one random person who takes us in! And we realize goodness was never in the places we thought it was! It was all along in the most humble of places: bound up in the heart of a true friend.

Adamantine

(adj.) From the Greek "αδαμαστος" meaning: "untameable"; used to describe the unbreakable.

(n.) A legendary substance or metal that is unbreakable; Virgil describes this material in the archaic writing *Aeneid book VI.*

Don't be afraid of your fears. They're not there to scare you. They're there to let you know that something is worth it.

"In case you never get a second chance: don't be afraid!"

"And what if you do get a second chance?"

"You take it!"

"What does it mean if I'm afraid? Does it mean something bad is going to happen?"

"No, it doesn't mean something bad is going to happen. It just means that you have the chance to be brave."

To know a species, look at its fears. To know yourself, look at your fears. Fear in itself is not important but fear stands there and points you in the direction of things that are important. Don't be afraid of your fears, they're not there to scare you; they're there to let you know that something is worth it.

Men have two greatest fears: the first fear is the fear of being needed and the second fear is the fear of not being needed.

"You shouldn't feel so bad about being afraid of so many things."

"Why not?"

"Because if you weren't afraid never ever, then you couldn't be brave never ever."

I tell people not to be afraid of their fears because their fears are not there to scare them; they're there to let them know that something is worth it. Yet I am often afraid. I guess that means in my life, lots of things have been worth it!

A lot of pieces I have written have to do with courage. As a result, people think that I am naturally brave. But what people don't know is that I grew up with phobias and many fears. I was scared of everything. So, I write of courage not because I have not known fear, but I write of courage because I have walked with fear but I have made the choice not to fear it.

We are fast moving into something, we are fast flung into something like asteroids cast into space by the death of a planet, we the people of earth are cast into space like burning asteroids and if we wish not to disintegrate into nothingness we must begin to now hold onto only the things that matter while letting go of all that doesn't. For when all of our dust and ice deteriorates into the cosmos, we will be left only with ourselves and nothing else. So if you want to be there in the end, today is the day to start holding onto your children, holding onto your loved ones, onto those who share your soul. Harbor and anchor into your heart: justice, truth, courage, bravery, belief, a firm vision, and a steadfast and sound mind. Be the person of meaningful and valuable thoughts. Don't look to the left, don't look to the right; we simply don't have the time. Never be afraid of fear.

When the demons start coming out—that's when you're nearing the light! It's hard for cockroaches to stay put without all the shadows. So in that case, keep on going!

The conception of each star was at the point of no return, of a desperate soul struggling to master the winds!

A star falls from the sky and into your hands. Then it seeps through your veins and swims inside your blood and becomes every part of you. And then you have to put it back into the sky. And it's the most painful thing you'll ever have to do and that you've ever done. But what's yours is yours. Whether it's up in the sky or here in your hands. And one day, it'll fall from the sky and hit you in the head real hard and that time, you won't have to put it back in the sky again.

Scripturient

(adj.) Having a violent desire to write.

Writing, music, sculpting, painting and prayer! These are the three things that are most closely related! Writers, musicians, sculptors, painters and the faithful are the ones who make things out of nothing. Everybody else make things out of something, they have materials! But a written work can be done with nothing, it can begin in the soul! A musical piece begins with a harmony in the soul, a sculpture begins with a formless, useless piece of rock chiseled and formed and molded into the thing that was first conceived in the sculptor's heart! A painting can be carried inside the mind for a lifetime, before ever being put onto paper or canvas! And a prayer! A prayer is a thought, a remembrance, a whisper and a communion that is from the soul going to what cannot be seen, yet it can move mountains! And so I believe that these five things are interrelated, these five kinds of people are kin.

People have many cruel expectations from writers. People expect novelists to live on a hill with three kids and a spouse, people expect children's storywriters to never have sex, and people expect all great poets to be dead.

And these are all very difficult expectations to fulfill, I think.

I hope I don't write *too* many books! When I look at authors who have written too many books, I wonder to myself "When did they live?" I certainly want to write *because* I live! I know I don't want to write in order to live! My writing is an overflow of the wine glass of my life; not a basin in which I wash out my ideals and expectations.

Perhaps writing is the ability to breathe under water, or something like that. We swim underwater and we're all supposed to drown, but some of us write and because of that, we sprout gills so we can breathe! But then that would mean we watch everyone else die. Let me think about that a minute. I think that writers *do* watch everyone else die. What a funny and sad thing!

Fiction is written with reality and reality is written with fiction. We can write fiction because there is reality and we can write reality because there is fiction; everything we consider today to be myth and legend, our ancestors believed to be history and everything in our history includes myths and legends. Before the splendid modern-day mind was formed, our cultures and civilizations were conceived in the wombs of, and born of, what we identify today as "fiction, unreality, myth, legend, fantasy, folklore, imaginations, fabrications and tall tales." And in our suddenly realized glory of all our modern-day "advancements" we somehow fail to ask ourselves the question "Who designated myths and legends as unreality?" But I ask myself this question because who decided that he was spectacular enough to stand up and say to our ancestors: "You were all stupid and disillusioned and imagining things" and then why did we all decide to believe this person? There are many realities; not just one. There is a truth that goes far beyond what we are told today to believe in. And we find that truth when we are brave enough to break away from what keeps everybody else feeling comfortable. Your reality is what you believe in. And nobody should be able to tell you to believe otherwise.

To those who think that being an author and publisher is not work, I say to you: Try writing something, then try getting people to read it, then try getting people to like it, then try getting people to love it, then try publishing what you've done, then try marketing what you've published, then try getting people to buy what you've put on the market. When you have done all of these things successfully, then you can come back to me and tell me if it isn't called work.

Love Notes

"I have no words for you... I have never met you before but reading your updates are a great nourishment in my life... I get so uplifted 'n build an unshakeable attitude I never had... I appreciate my life even more 'cause am the one who makes it... you are so blessed... You don't know how many people's hearts you touch with your inspiring words."

~ *Olivrine Zarine Bwire,* Kenya

"Your ethereal logic is somehow cohesive, I think you are a step above better than awesome."

~ *Tom Blumm,* Maui

"C. JoyBell C., I would like to thank you for sharing your writings. They are phenomenal and wonderfully raw. Just beautiful. They have touched me and propelled me into fully accepting that yes I am human, yes I am a young growing woman and hell yes I owe it to myself to live fully, gracefully and honestly."

~ *Kendra Hale,* Seattle

"I absolutely love your work..."

~ *Lori Sawicky Puskas*, Pennsylvania

"Thanks for all the wonderful words you have shared with us!"

~ *Vidur Mahadeo*, Newcastle, South Africa

"I find your writings so inspiring."

~ *Tamara Ní Mhaoileoin,* Ireland

"I'm becoming so beautiful that your writings shine once more in my heart!!!!!!!"

"Forever shine on my heart!!!!"

~ *Ariel Adamo,* Buenos Aires, Argentina

"I recently started to read your quotes and admire them so much. I was at a memorial service over the weekend in Brockton, MA, and had to deliver a tribute on behalf of my organization, but since I knew I had this task to perform, I had been wondering as to what to say to the bereaved family to comfort them and give them courage as they endure the healing process. I quoted two of my favorite quotations of yours and they seemed to fit the occasion very well. You are an inspiring writer. Nice to connect with you on Facebook."

~ *Sam Slewion,* Pennsylvania

"I like everything about you."

~ *Funyanwa Hoyo*, Cape Town

"Your writings truly enriched my life. It has given me so much understanding about myself. Also why people behave the way they do. It helps me to heal and to feel more free to be myself. Stay beautiful and blessed. Thank you."

~ *Mapuii Zothanpuii*, New Delhi, India

"You are a sage, mythical creature. Never stop dancing with your words."

~ *Poe Macabrette*, Ireland

"You understand time, space, matter, and energy so well...Wow! You are the Universal Mother! You are the Universe!"

~ *Jayanta Sarkar*, Bangladore, India

"I am so glad. In finding you today I found me. I've been in tears ever since."

~ *David Bilman*, L.A.

"Just found you... already love you..."

~ *Malissia Woodall*, Seattle

"Loved your quotes I came across accidentally. The last quotes I loved were from Virginia Satir and that was a long time back."

~ *Roshni Saghal*, Pune, Maharashtra, India

"Thank you for always having the perfect things to say!"

~ *Nichole Kirk*, Texas

"Hi! I love your quotes! I hope you continue to show your greatness to the world! If there were more people in this world with the ability to look at things the way some people do in this world (like you) then it would be allot better place."

~ *Maxwell Alexander*

"I live by your quotes, they make me smile. Am anxious to read your work!"

~ *Vastine Bondurant,* Texas

"I just wanted to say that everyday I find a quote of yours that just makes me want to shout *that is me!!*"

~ *Kristie Alverson,* Alpine, Utah

"My heart grew into it's big girl clothes and is wearing them like a queen since discovering your poems. Thank you."

~ *Renee Airya*, Scottsdale, Arizona

"You have a unique, intelligent and beautiful mind. I enjoy reading your stuff!"

~ *Angela Cotellessa*, Virginia

"Good day ma'am. I always love to read your inspirational quotes. It always gives me inspiration in everyday life. Thank you so much."

~ *Benjie Joson Balane*, Bulacan, Philippines

"Your writing talents are amazing! For me, it is like surfing an ambidextrous brain wave. Very rare... the left brain is writing rationally, logically... very planned and structured, while at the same time the right brain is writing intuitively... very fluid, spontaneous, artistic... always imaginative and a bit elusive...The results... A wild, fun ride and one that also makes you think and ponder the larger, more serious questions of life..."

~ *Lynda Herbert Parrott*, New Orleans

"What an inspiring lady you are, Joy!"

~ *Johnson Kansiime,* Uganda

"I feel like the words you write come straight from my spirit and onto the paper. Thank you for writing me, and I'm sure so many other wonderfully restless women."

~ *Christina Rae Coolidge,* Canada

"Ever since I discovered you I visit your page (Facebook) every day! I love your words... they make me think, escape and reconsider about things that I didn't wanna see before... looking forward to reading your books too..."

~ *Dimitra Apatsidis,* London, UK

"Wonderful! I am a fan!"

~ *Mark Hewer,* Windsor, Ontario, Canada

"Thank you... It is so rare to find a writer who approaches the world with not only depth and insight but who also writes in such a way as to embrace human fallibility. It makes such a refreshing change to read something not only inspiring but real."

~ *Tamaryn Moss,* South Africa

"Just wanted to say that *you* are the *best* writer *in my* opinion. I mean your quotes are really amazing and I love reading them. Your writing style, the way you express your feelings in words are too awesome. I don't think that there is any other writer out there who can do the same!"

~ *Appy Thapliyal,* India

"Amazing. Inspirational. Feminine. Powerful. Eloquent. Your words inspire me! *A viaxe continúa!*"

~ *Connie Baña*

"You know, you've been one of my favorite persons for awhile. If I could obtain your new book, with a signature, well, I don't have the right word for it just yet."

"Okay — So I really like what you say. I don't think I have disagreed with anything you've said thus far... I even used you as a Philosopher for my Philosophy project in school. It was on perfection, and you had a well-founded and brilliant idea on it."

~ *Stephen Isnor*

"I very much enjoy your insights. I discovered you today and I feel very fortunate to be in the right place at the right time. My best to you."

"Thank you for being."

~ *Rick Johnson,* Minnesota

"Dear madam, you are truly amazing and you inspire me so much, your works are truly motivating... in my world people think I'm carefree, fun and always happy but the truth is I'm a mess!!!! But your words help me in lots of ways, thank you... keep doing what you do, my support is with you always!!!"

~ *Cindii Ozukum*

"Your words are so magically uplifting!"

~ *Jake Evans,* Mauritius

"Your words inspire me... So grateful to have found your writings!"

~ *Silvana Sepe Tuweri,* Neuss, Germany

"Just beautiful... your work touches me immensely. Thank you for sharing your soul and bringing such beautiful light to others."

~ *Sheila Correia,* Chicago

"I wanted to write to you to say I love your writing, your words touch me, make me cry, make me smile... I'm using your words to help me stay strong whilst struggling at the moment... Thank you x"

~ *Candice Smith*, London

"Today I realized what it is I enjoy so much about your writing and why I will continue to share and promote it. It's all about awareness and acceptance. You don't tell us to love everyone and be "good" all the time. People dismiss that out of hand because it's impossible. You tell us to love ourselves then love what we love and walk away from what we don't. You don't tell us everything is beautiful— if we can only see the beauty. You tell us to see it all and if it's beautiful we will feel it without having to put a label on it. The world needs that. We need to know it's okay to be imperfect. The acceptance of what we judge as imperfect is enough to stop a war."

"It's the middle of the night here— one of those that you wake up nearly dead and wonder if anything will ever reignite the internal spark that makes life interesting. I opened one of your books... and the fire, it burst forth dancing, consuming the decay and promising more adventures. Many, many thanks."

~ *Donna G. Kirkland*

"I AM YOUR GREATEST FAN. You have brought positivism in my life. Thank you so much."

~ *Smrity Bhattarai,* Kathmandu, Nepal

"I didn't know much about you, until a few minutes ago. I went through a few of your inspirational quotes at Goodreads! Oh, and how they healed my soul!!"

~ *Ananya Deori,* India

"I have been in love with your work for quite some time now. Your words are powerful, meaningful and beautiful, I find myself quoting you on my FB page constantly! You are an inspiration!"

~ *Alexa Helibron Ortiz*, Miami, Florida

"I am in love with all of your work. You have become such an inspiration for me. I am actually going to get a quote of yours tattooed on my side... my ribcage... this summer."

~ *Alanah Burge*, Texas

"I have decided that I am going to gift myself a bottle of perfume! All because of your words... thank you!"

~ *Aritri Das*

"I feel like you are a dear friend."

~ *Maria Dominguez- Roberts,* New York

"How your words speak to me when I want to speak to no one... Thank you!"

~ *Rathika Rajoo*

"I've been reading some of your mind's thoughts on digitized paper. Excellent stuff! Thanks for sharing your mind."

~ *Charlie Killswitch Van Eperen*

"Thank you for your beautiful writing, it has been a comfort to me recently."

~ *Dr. Charlene Spencer*

"Did you know that you have helped me to become a better woman every time you write such Amazing quotes... Thank you for being you and Thank you for sharing your quotes... May God always be with you dear... Love."

~ *Inge Nathalia*

"Your words are incredible... are there any live interviews with you on camera? Would love to hear you speak..."

"I am so smitten by your beautiful words."

~ *Caroline Duval,* Montreal, Canada

"You have the most amazing quotes ever!!!!"

~ *Eleni Amvrosiatos,* Adelaide, Australia

"Your writings and quotes on Perfume / Fragrances and Life are brilliant and have been worthy of The Perfume Foundation to inspire and include on a number of occasions."

~ *Paul K. Holmes,* Vice Chairman and CEO of International Perfume Foundation

"I just love you! Thanks for being!"

~ *Marsha Hall*

"I was intrigued by a quote that a friend wrote which was one of yours and then I came upon the beauty of words so beautifully strung together that it reminded me of the garlands I used to make for my mom when I was a kid. Then I came upon your website and from there the Facebook page. The feeling was as if I had suddenly found the treasure that I had been looking for."

~ *Uzma Khan,* Pakistan

"Just wanted to say that I LOVE your writing and quote you often. I am a big fan."

~ *Tom Gordon*

"I love your quotes JoyBell... very insightful and original."

~ *Erik Madsen*, Copenhagen, Denmark

"Your message is so calming."

~ *Murari Barnwal*, India

"It's one thing to write the truth and its another thing to write beautifully, but to write the truth beautifully is the rarest gift of all."

~ *Arman Matthews*, Kansas

"I can't stop reading, re-reading, liking and loving your words!!! I can see a part of me in every single word!! I was, am and will always be one of your biggest fans!! Keep it up! You rock!!!"

~ *Dr. Josette Koborsy*, Lebanon

"I just want to say *Thank You!* Your work is truly helping me through a very difficult and painful point in my life... you are an inspiration! God Bless You!!"

~ *Angela Renee Jeffries*, North Carolina

"I like you. I like you a lot."

~ *Nicole Yakira*

"Beautiful, wacky and heartfelt. I love it!"

~ *Gene Powers*, Rome, Georgia

"You are such an amazing writer. Thank you for sharing your insights with the rest of the world."

~ *Jodi Mayday*

"Thanks for throwing yourself out there. I am posting your quote on my vision board. Crazy BEAUTIFUL!!!"

~ *Nicole De La Montagne,* Winnipeg, Manitoba, Canada

"Thank you for your creativity and perspective on life."

~ *Martha Williams*

"So glad to find your unique insights and ageless wisdom!"

~ *Susan Harden*

"You have amazing, interesting, meaningful, inspiring thoughts..."

~ *Emma Harrison*, Melbourne, Australia

"Your stuff is so beautiful and helpful! Thank you!"

~ *Avalon McCoy*, Ontario, Canada

"I found you by chance today on Facebook. A writer I follow on Twitter quotes you often. You have such insight and wisdom on life. Are you on Twitter? You could reach so many people who need a word of encouragement in their darkness: some laughter, someone who understands. A voice for what we all feel deep down inside. We all have a story."

~ *Marcia Wyman Hug*, Connecticut

"You inspire me... Thank you!"

~ *Ekene Nezerem,* Nigeria

"Love your writing. Don't stop."

~ *Clarisse Chin,* Perth, Western Australia

"Beautiful inside and out... thank you for being an inspiration. You brought a lot of positivity in my life. God bless you more!"

~ *Hannelie Varona Baldomar Bonete,* Philippines

"The written word is such a powerful medium... in its purest form it can be mystical and magical, ethereal and surreal, inspirational and transformational... you have that quintessential quality to transport your readers to another dimension in a style that is uniquely yours... an authentic simplicity with an underlying profundity that truly defines poetry in motion. Thank you for being such a positive light force in an ever-increasing dark world."

~ *Carrie Gupte*, Trinidad and Tobago

"I am truly captivated. I admire how your mind, heart and soul are beautifully expressed by your words. You have such a beautiful gift. Thanks for sharing your gift to all of us! Can't wait to get a copy of your books!"

~ *Jenalyn Dones Agalla*, Zhengzhou, China

"Your spirit and you ability to combine the essence of the unwritten soul with words is nothing short of incredible. I am deeply moved. I stumbled on your quotes on

Goodreads and just kept reading them... During and after moments of personal spiritual enlightenment I have said to myself "If only I could find the words to express what I am feeling right now!" And my... you have found a lot of those words!"

~ *Eroc Arroyo-Montano,*
Massachusetts

"You are such an inspiration to me!!!! I love all of your quotes!! They keep me motivated and give me a positive outlook on life!!"

~ *Lonella Jones,* Bel-Air, Maryland

"Firstly just to say I hate poetry, however, I have just read one of your poems and you have no idea how it has blessed my day and helped me in a healing process which has taken many years, your art is truly from a divine place and I too, am a mermaid. Thank you. xx"

~ *Luke Wilson*

"Deep truth! Thank you!"

~ *Scott Wright*

"You are absolutely brilliant! I feel every word you write. Don't ever change. xx"

~ *Rebekah Rowsey*, Indiana

"I am so inspired by you, you are amazing... the things you write really opens my soul!"

~ *Mikhe Coetzee*, Pretoria, South Africa

"Oh my god! I read a few of your quotes yesterday and I love them all! I'm planning on getting one of them tattooed! You are something special and you have a gift! I'm glad I found your quotes!"

~ *Dana J. Del Torro*, Beaumont, California

"I love you work... I get lost in it... x"

~ *Magda Brzezinska,* Stafford, England, UK

"Love what you say and the simplicity with which you reach across."

~ *Rachna Sharma Sirtaj,* Munich, Germany

"I think I found a new friend, your writings touch my soul, I thank you."

~ *Linda D'Agostino*

"Beautiful thoughts, truly. I know I'll walk around today carrying your inspiration."

~ *Roselle Quin,* Philippines

"Hello, I wanted to thank you for following me (on Twitter) I think you're such an inspiration and your quotes always inspire me to want more and to be myself and enjoy life! Not a lot have that amazing quality; you're definitely someone I'd like to be like when I grow up! Love, from Romania. xx"

~ *Angie,* Romania

"I truly admire you and your work. I think you're a beautiful human being filled with pure light and magic. Keep on being so wonderful and never stop dreaming and sharing your inner light, I just really wanted to thank you for a lot of inspiration and good vibes. Wishing you the best always. xx Adi"

~ *Adi Dekel,* Israel

"Hi, my name is Maaike, I'm a 17- year- old girl from Belgium. I'm currently into reading and writing and I really, really love your work. The past months have been really difficult for me, however, I didn't want to send you a message about my problems; I just wanted to let you know that your quotes and poems have helped me a lot when I felt down. Your work makes me smile, makes me cry and most of all makes me want to write, myself! That is the support your writing gives me. I have searched for your books, but I can't find them in the stores here, but I will keep looking or search them online. I'm a huge fan of yours and wish you all the best. With love, Maaike xxx"

~ *Maaike,* Belgium

"Thank you for your wise words! Your quotes are keeping me sane and centered... not easy... How lovely to be able to send you a message of thanks."

~ *Caro Nijeboer*, Netherlands

"Huge fan. I'm pursuing a career change to help others via music therapy. The odds are against me but your writing keeps me inspired."

"I also wanted to share that I am in addiction recovery and your quotes (esp. about being your own critic) have helped me respect my life. So thank you very much. Improving my self-esteem has helped me in recovery to become all I can be — which is more than I would've guessed! ... My life is so much better these days, I have joy. You are very gifted! A lot of your words have a way of bringing life to the spirit and soul. This is what people in recovery need, and that's how you help us! I am dedicated now in giving back what was freely given to me so that I can reach others and serve those who need it most."

~ *Mike Hansen*, Milwaukee, WI

"You are f*****g ACE! I love you!!!"

"The effect you've had on myself and other people's lives has been astronomical... you are so loved by many!!! You are in every sense of the word the "TRUTH" and if anyone is stupid enough to think otherwise, they should go and fart peas at the moon!!"

~ *Richard Willems*, Nottingham, England

"I look at your writing as a gift from God, to me. I believe in miracles, and I believe your words contribute to some of the miracles that happen in my life. Your words have guided me in times of need. They have helped me to rethink decisions and choices that could have brought me down an old path from the past, which I never want to go back to. It is like the world stops, and as if they are being directly spoken to me when I read you. I have prayed about and meditated on many issues in my life, and after one particular troublesome occasion, I discovered your writing. It was just what I needed to see in that exact moment. It was no coincidence. There is a saying, "Coincidences are God's way of remaining anonymous." I believe that in my time of need, my prayers were answered and I was lead to your words by God. I now continue to refer to them often when I want to seek inspiration. Your writing is a timeless treasure to me that I will look at over and over again. I am so grateful that you care about people the way you do and how you choose to share with us. You have helped me a lot."

"Your words stimulate my mind and open me up to beautiful things. They take me away from the chatter in my mind that causes anxiety. It is like being surrounded by nature. Never, have I enjoyed reading so much and the great thing is, your work is timeless. For me, you are like "the

Beatles of writing." It will never get stale and the meanings will reveal more to me each time I read them."

~ *Mark Buggy*, Kingston, Ontario, Canada

My grandmother always used to tell me, that her mother always used to tell her: "Never say goodbye, only say farewell." And so instead of saying "The end" right now, I will say "Goodnight" instead.

Acknowledgments

Wonderful reader, I would like to acknowledge *you,* for allowing me to become a beautiful part of your life, through my words thrice shared. The revelation process could not have been completed without your discovery of me and the treasures that are mine to share. I think that the process begins even before anything is revealed to you; it begins when the seeds of thought are first born in the soil of my mind and bloom in the sunlight of my heart. That is the first revelation, the first "sharing." The second comes when these living words are passed on to another, by which the revealed thing then becomes discovered and it is by this discovery done by you, that my own words have been able to reveal themselves all over again, to me. They become like the infantile seeds they once were: small but containing a universe of light. They come back to me as a third revelation and I eat of their fruit! This *Vade Mecum* is a gathering of those fruits. But it hasn't stopped there! By sharing my gathered fruits with you, that have already been thrice revealed through myself and through the world— it becomes a revelation for a fourth time! Four cornerstones complete this process, and I thank *you* for joining on the final leg of it!

I thank my difficult experiences in life that put me in the places where I could bear these seeds within myself. I also thank the best and most beautiful and happy experiences in my life, that have done the same! However, I would like to formally say *goodbye* to difficulty as a teacher. I don't want you as a teacher, anymore!

Yilkee Lam, thank you so much for your relentless assistance with the layout of this book! I would have gone half mad without your help! facebook.com/YilkeePhotography

Thank you, Herb Mallette, for the very first proper review of my novella, *Saint Paul Trois Châteaux: 1948*. And thank you so much for agreeing to write a foreword for *Vade Mecum*— I am most grateful!

To the individuals who have been there for me through thick and thin— thank you.

Notes

Notes

The main typeface of this book is presented to you in mostly 14 pt. Garamond, a font named after the French punch-cutter, Claude Garamond (c. 1480–1561). Claude Garamond came to prominence in the 1540s, first for a Greek typeface he was commissioned to create for the French king, Francis I, to be used in a series of books by Robert Estienne. When Claude Garamond died in 1561, his punches and matrices were sold to Christophe Plantin, in Antwerp, which enabled the Garamond fonts to be used on many printers. This version became very popular in Europe.

The only complete set of the original Garamond dyes and matrices is at the *Plantin-Moretus Museum*, in Antwerp, Belgium.

Garamond's letterforms convey a sense of fluidity and consistency. It has also been noted to be one of the most eco-friendly major fonts when it comes to ink usage.